North Dakota

North Dakota

Martin Hintz

Children's Press®
A Division of Grolier Publishing
New York   London   Hong Kong   Sydney
Danbury, Connecticut

Frontispiece: Little Missouri River

Front cover: Sculpted Badland formations,
Theodore Roosevelt National Park

Back cover: Maltese Cross cabin, Theodore Roosevelt National Park

Consultant: Janet Daily, *North Dakota History Magazine*

Please note: All statistics are as up-to-date as possible at the time of publication.

Visit Children's Press on the Internet at http://publishing.grolier.com

Book production by Editorial Directions, Inc.

Library of Congress Cataloging-in-Publication Data

Hintz, Martin.
   North Dakota / Martin Hintz.
      144 p. 24 cm. — (America the beautiful. Second series)
   Includes bibliographical references and index.
   Summary: Describes the geography, plants, animals, history, economy, religions, cul-
ture, sports, arts, and people of North Dakota.
   ISBN 0-516-21072-6
   1. North Dakota—Juvenile literature. [1. North Dakota] 1. Title. II. Series.
F636.3.H56 2000
978.4'21—dc21
                                         99-042902
                                                CIP
                                                AC

GROLIER
PUBLISHING

Acknowledgments

The author would like to thank the staff of the North Dakota secretary of state, the North Dakota Department of Natural Resources, the North Dakota Tourism Department, the United States Forest Service, and the many North Dakotans who took the time to answer questions and provide background material. They included farmers, performers, kids on bikes, livestock dealers, doctors, businesswomen, tribal officers, writers, hotel clerks, bus drivers, and fair organizers.

Badlands

Sunflowers

Bentonite hills

Contents

Western
meadowlark

Little Missouri River

Medora

Sledding

Purple coneflowers

CHAPTER ONE

Land of Horizons

During the summer in North Dakota, endless rolling fields of sunflowers, wheat, and corn seem to become one with the horizon. As writer Roger C. Kennedy said of the area, "If only we climbed a stepladder, we could see a hundred miles." Perhaps it is fitting that the world's largest buffalo can be found in North Dakota—in the shape of a three-story statue overlooking the city of Jamestown in southeast North Dakota. Cattle now graze on the prairie where herds of buffalo once thundered.

The changing seasons in North Dakota are also dramatic. On raw winter days, the wind howls with a vengeance, pushing great drifts of snow over the open prairie. The long dreary months can seem to go on forever. But when spring finally arrives, bringing melting snow and early rains, new vegetation turns purple, blue, and pink. By summer, the golden crops can be dazzling. With

North Dakota is known for its dramatic open spaces.

Opposite: Sunset over a prairie wetland

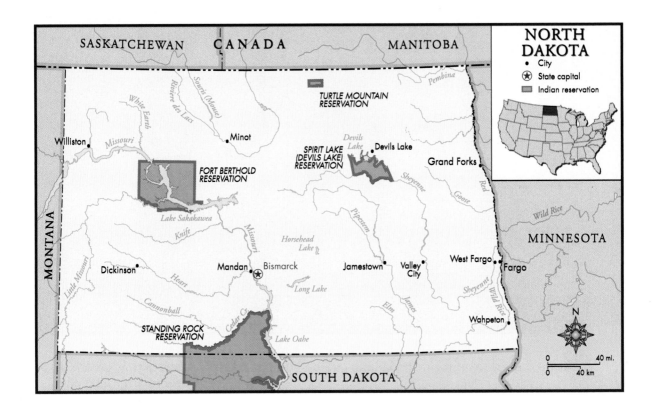

SASKATCHEWAN   CANADA   MANITOBA

TURTLE MOUNTAIN
RESERVATION

Rivière des Lacs
Souris (Mouse)
White Earth
Missouri
Williston•   Minot•
Pembina

Devils
Lake
SPIRIT LAKE   •Devils Lake
(DEVILS LAKE)
RESERVATION

Grand Forks•

FORT BERTHOLD
RESERVATION

Lake Sakakawea
Knife
Missouri
Little Missouri

Horsehead
Lake

Sheyenne
Goose
Red

MINNESOTA

Wild Rice

Pipestem

Dickinson•   Heart
Mandan• Bismarck
(★)   Long Lake
Jamestown•   Valley
City•
West Fargo•
•Fargo
Sheyenne
Wild Rice
James
Elm

MONTANA

Cannonball
Cedar Cr.
STANDING ROCK
RESERVATION   Lake Oahe
Wahpeton•

N

SOUTH DAKOTA

0   40 mi.
0   40 km

**Geopolitical map
of North Dakota**

autumn comes a rainbow explosion of colors from stands of oaks,
maples, willows, and beeches. A fresh crisp snap in the air predicts
nastier weather, and the cycle begins anew.

The weather has molded the people of North Dakota, tough-
ening them with its roughness but also ensuring their openness of
spirit. The citizens have to cope with whatever nature throws their
way—tornadoes, floods, droughts, or blizzards—but it is balanced
with the beauty and expansiveness of the land. The sheer immen-
sity of earth and sky encourages reflective thought and leads to a
better understanding of life's important issues, such as preserving
the water, soil, and air.

**Opposite: Winter often
brings lots of snow to
North Dakota.**

CHAPTER TWO

The First Dakotans

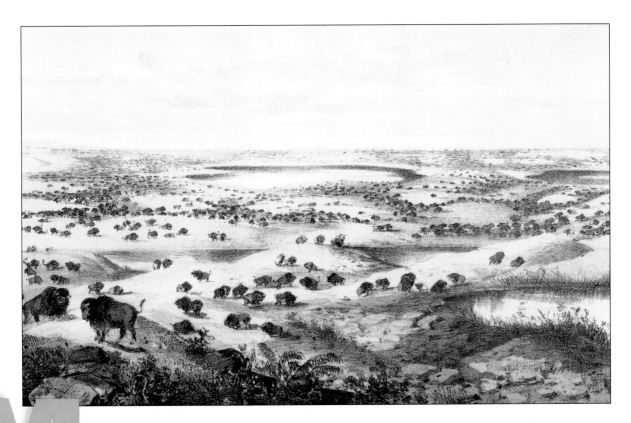

Bison once roamed the North Dakota landscape.

More than 12,000 years ago, sheets of ice covered almost all of upper North America. The weight of the glaciers crushed and flattened the land. What is now the state of North Dakota was part of this vast frozen landscape. Yet on the forward fringes of the ice pack was a lush, fertile world inhabited by elephant-like mammoths and huge bison. They grazed across rich grasslands fed by streams created by melting ice packs.

Hunters also found their way to the edge of the glaciers. These Paleo-Indians were probably descendants of early people who struggled across a land bridge that then existed between Asia and North America. Research in the 1990s indicates that some of North America's first inhabitants may also have come from Europe or the Pacific Islands.

Opposite: Bentonite hills in Theodore Roosevelt National Park

Wherever their place of origin in those long-ago ages, the first Dakotans were skilled hunters. Evidence of their presence has been found by archaeologists digging around New Town and many other sites in North Dakota. Stone chips, rudimentary tools, and spear points from several eras have been discovered throughout what is now North Dakota.

As these nomads traveled across the vast stretches of upper North America, they gathered fruits and nuts to supplement their diet of meat. As the centuries passed, the early people disappeared or were absorbed into the next wave of newcomers to inhabit the area. By 600 B.C., mound-building farmers lived in North Dakota, around present-day Devils Lake. Some of their mounds, perhaps used for religious purposes, can still be seen.

First Native Americans

By the 1400s, North Dakota was a transition land for several Native American nations. However, when the first Europeans arrived in the 1700s, probably fewer than 100,000 Indians were living there. These Native Americans felt a kinship with all living things, holding similar beliefs about the creation of Earth and their place in the world.

The Mandan were the first contemporary Indians to live in North Dakota. They grew corn and tobacco. Archaeologists believe the early Mandan journeyed north along the Missouri River from territories to the south. Ancient campsites unearthed along that route have yielded artifacts showing how this Indian nation evolved.

A Mandan chief

An earthen lodge in a preserved Mandan village

The Mandan lived in earthen lodges along the Missouri River. Warm in the winter and cool in the summer, their homes were located close to the water for fishing and irrigating crops. Although the Mandan were primarily farmers, they also hunted buffalo.

The Arikara and Hidatsa also lived there. But as early as the 1600s, some members of their tribe journeyed farther and farther afield in search of wild game, and returned less often to the villages of their origins. Some believe that the Hidatsa who journeyed westward into Montana and the Rocky Mountain foothills evolved into the Crow nation.

Other Indian peoples in North Dakota, such as the Cheyenne and Cree, lived in one place for most of the spring and summer and traveled to warmer areas in the autumn and winter. The Chippewa were forest people who traveled west out of Minnesota to settle along the Turtle Mountain and Pembina Gorge areas of northeastern North Dakota.

The Dakota, or Sioux, and the Assiniboine followed the buffalo. They lived in tepees that were easily packed and transported on a

Life in a Mandan village

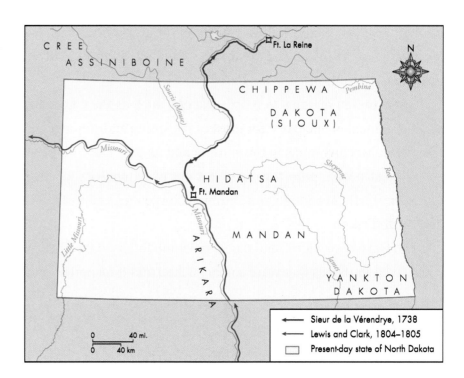

Exploration of North Dakota

travois—a platform supported by two poles tied to a horse and dragged on the ground. The Dakota were the best-known Indian group of North Dakota. They had an advanced democratic society that elected the bravest and noblest warriors as their village leaders. The Dakota called themselves the *Oceti Sakowin*, or "Seven Council Fires," a reference to their seven tribal units.

The Importance of the Horse

Native Americans were introduced to horses as early as the 1500s. At first, they captured the animals in raids on the Spaniards in the Southwest. Eventually, they raised their own horses.

A horse was a valuable commodity on the plains. Horses enabled Indian groups to travel far distances. The Indians subsequently developed a far-flung trading system. They traded skins and dried meat for shells from the Gulf of Mexico, copper from the Great Lakes, and obsidian—a hard stone used for knives and other implements—from the Rocky Mountains. These Indian communities in North Dakota also formed alliances when necessary to protect their lands from outsiders such as the Shoshone to the south and the Blackfeet to the north.

Early Exploration

Soon white explorers came onto the scene. In 1731, a Canadian fur trader named Pierre Gaultier de Varennes, Sieur de La Vérendrye, led an expedition into unexplored parts of Canada, north of present-day North Dakota. He had heard about a mighty river that flowed westward and hoped to find a water route to the Pacific Ocean.

On October 18, 1738, La Vérendrye ventured out of the trading post of Fort La Reine in Canada and entered what is now North Dakota. Traveling with a group of whites and Assiniboine, La Vérendrye came across a Mandan village near today's Bismarck. It was cold and snowy, so he stayed with the Mandan for two weeks before returning to Fort La Reine, without having found a waterway to the west. But La Vérendrye's reports circulated widely around the West as well as in the East and encouraged other exploration.

In 1797, David Thompson, a surveyor for the North West Company, was sent to map the region and trace the 49th parallel—the official boundary between Canada and the new United States. On the journey, which eventually covered 50,000 miles (80,450 kilo-

Dakota's First Trading Post

Alexander Henry established the first permanent trading post in North Dakota in 1801. His outpost at Pembina was in the northeastern tip of what is now North Dakota. There, he planted exten- sive gardens and grew potatoes, beets, onions, and other vegeta- bles. Alexander Henry's writings are among the best accounts we have of life along this rugged frontier. ■

meters), he visited numerous Mandan villages along the upper Missouri River.

In 1803, the United States purchased a vast stretch of territory in the west-central United States from France. The acquisition was called the Louisiana Purchase. President Thomas Jefferson wanted to know what was in this sprawling land of prairie and mountain. He asked his secretary, Meriwether Lewis, and Lewis's former army commander, William Clark, to explore and map the area. Their expedition left St. Louis on May 14, 1804.

The men journeyed up the Missouri River and reached central North Dakota by October 1804. There they constructed Fort Mandan on the east bank of the river, now a historical site. The Lewis and Clark party stayed at Fort Mandan until April 1805, and then struck out across the plains, reaching the Pacific Ocean in November 1805. They returned to North Dakota in August 1806. Their round-trip ended in St. Louis on September 23, 1806, after covering 8,000 miles (12,874 km). Their precise scientific observations

Fort Mandan is now a historic site.

Sacajawea

A Shoshone woman named Sacajawea (sometimes spelled Sakakawea) was hired as a scout and interpreter for the Lewis and Clark expedition. She had been kidnapped as a youngster and raised by the Hidatsa.

Only sixteen years old, Sacajawea guided the explorers across the plains, through the Rocky Mountains, and on to the Pacific coast. When Lewis and Clark reached Sacajawea's original home in the Rocky Mountains, they found her brother, who was now a tribal leader. He loaned them horses and other guides to help them cross the mountains and return safely. During the journey, Sacajawea also helped find edible roots and berries, treated the sick, and even saved the expedition's papers and scientific instruments when one of their canoes capsized.

Sacajawea was the wife of Toussaint Charbonneau, a French-Canadian interpreter at Fort Mandan. She traveled with her husband and their infant son, Jean Baptiste, on the journey.

North Dakota named its largest lake, Lake Sakakawea, after Sacajawea. A statue of Sacajawea and her son stands on the state capitol grounds in Bismarck (left). The U.S. government has honored her contributions to the explorations by putting her image on the new $1 coin minted in 1999. ■

and recordings of plants and wildlife helped identify hundreds of new species of flora and fauna in the Missouri River area.

The Fur Trade

Fur trading was big business along the Canada–United States border in the first half of the 1800s. Thousands of animal skins were sent to the East Coast for shipment to Europe where they were made into expensive hats, coats, and blankets. John Jacob Astor started the American Fur Company, competing with the British-

The Métis Traders

The Métis people lived along the Pembina and Red Rivers. They spoke a mixture of French and Native American dialects. Métis men were easily recognized by the colorful sashes they wore around their waists. The enterprising Métis used lumbering carts (above) to haul goods to and from the frontier outposts. They transported furs and buffalo skins from their hub at St. Joseph (now Walhalla, North Dakota) to St. Paul, Minnesota, and returned with goods such as flour, anvils, and rocking chairs. ■

owned Hudson's Bay Company and the North West Company. Another American, Manuel Lisa, founded the Missouri Fur Company, which had several outposts in North Dakota.

Devastation for Native Americans

Sadly, the early explorers and fur traders also brought diseases to North America. In 1837, an epidemic of smallpox devastated

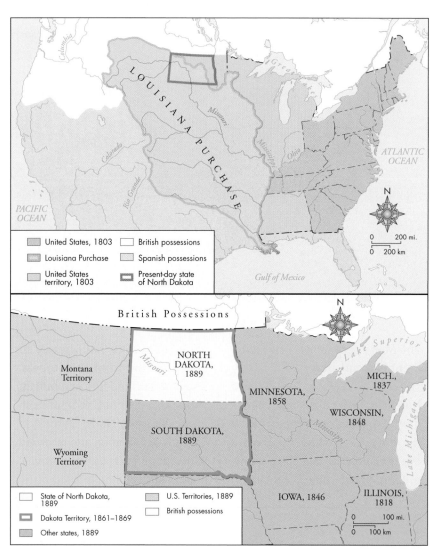

Historical map of North Dakota

North Dakota's Native American people, who had no immunity to the disease. The movement of white settlers into North Dakota also brought the slaughter of buffalo herds and the loss of traditional Indian hunting grounds. For Native Americans, buffalo were the source of their food, clothing, and shelter. In the second half of the 1800s, challenges to traditional life led to Indian resistance, battles, and the eventual assignment of Native Americans to reservations throughout North Dakota.

Settlement

As treaty agreements, backed by the U.S. Army, forced the Native Americans off their lands, more settlers poured into the region. Steamboats plied the Red River (unusual because it runs north) and the Missouri River, bringing newcomers ready to stake claims. The first such vessel to travel up the Red River was the *Anson Northrup*, named after the man who built the boat and finally got it upriver. Northrup won a $2,000 prize from merchants in St. Paul for his feat. Land-hungry farmers plowed and planted the fertile river valleys, often living in tar-paper shacks or sod huts until they could afford wood.

The *Anson Northrup* served people along the Red River.

By 1861, enough people lived in what are now North and South Dakota and most of Wyoming and Montana that political leaders there pushed for territory status. On March 2, 1861, President James Buchanan signed the Organic Act to provide "a temporary government for the Territory of Dakota." However, the final document included only the Dakotas.

President Abraham Lincoln, who succeeded Buchanan, appointed William Jayne as the first territorial governor. Nine other territorial governors, many of whom had little interest in the West, followed Jayne. They preferred the comforts of the East and often lobbied on behalf of businesses and railroads rather than their constituents: the Dakotans.

A homestead in the Red River valley

Two congressional acts contributed to the settlement of the Dakotas. The Homestead Act of 1862 gave free land to anyone who wanted to grow crops. At first, there were few takers. The difficult conditions and loneliness were enough to scare anyone off.

Railroads

Railroads were also seen as an important way to encourage settlement. The granting of a charter to the Northern Pacific Railroad in 1864 allowed the construction of a rail line from Minnesota to Puget Sound on the Washington coast. Congress gave the railroad more than 50 million acres (20 million hectares). The Northern Pacific reached Fargo by 1872, and Bismarck and the Missouri River by 1873, before money dried up.

Jay Cooke, a wealthy investor, stepped in to encourage others to pour millions of dollars into the project. In return, he was to receive a majority ownership in the railroad line. But Cooke's company went bankrupt, triggering a national economic depression in 1873.

Finally, in 1879, the Northern Pacific made it west of Bismarck. Building a bridge across the river was no easy task, but that railroad bridge still carries trains today. Until the bridge was completed, track was laid across the frozen Missouri River. One of the Northern Pacific's competitors was the St. Paul, Minneapolis & Manitoba Railroad owned by James J. Hill. This hard-driving business tycoon from St. Paul, Minnesota, changed his company's name to the Great Northern Railroad. By 1893, his tracks linked the Midwest with the Pacific Coast. When another national economic panic struck in that year, Hill bought

James J. Hill played a key role in the establishment of railroads in the Dakotas.

controlling interest in his rival company, the Northern Pacific.

The timing was perfect. Population in the Dakotas soared by more than 1,000 percent between 1878 and 1890, thanks to the influx of homesteaders arriving by train. The population increase justified an intensified drive toward statehood.

Statehood

During the 1880s, several attempts were made to admit Dakota Territory as a state. The railroads and the flour mills preferred territorial status because it gave them more control over politicians, who were often swayed with bribes. But in 1887, the territorial legislature asked that a vote be taken to split the territory because there were enough people to form two states. The northern part of Dakota had about 190,000 residents, while the southern portion had almost 350,000. Only 60,000 were required for statehood. The territory's voters approved the suggestion. Subsequently, Congress approved the Omnibus Bill of 1889, which called for constitutions from North and South Dakota, Montana, and Washington.

On July 4, 1889, North Dakota's constitutional convention began in Bismarck. It took delegates forty-five days to draft twenty articles for the state's first constitution. In October, the pleased electorate approved the document by a huge margin.

On November 2, 1889, President Benjamin Harrison placed two pieces of paper on his desk. One was approval for the state of North Dakota and the other for South Dakota. Harrison covered up any references to them when he signed the papers making them states, so nobody knows which state was the thirty-ninth state to join the Union and which was the fortieth. Officially, North Dakota came first because its name comes first alphabetically.

The new state's Native American population had other concerns. More than a year later, North Dakota was the site of a standoff between followers of Dakota leader Sitting Bull and the Indian police sent by the U.S. government to arrest him for encouraging revolt. On December 15, 1890, Sitting Bull and his son were killed on the Standing Rock Reservation.

President Benjamin Harrison signed the document that made North Dakota a state on November 2, 1889.

CHAPTER THREE

After Statehood

Land seekers
arriving by train in
North Dakota in 1898

North Dakota's railroads flourished during the last hours of territorial status and the first years after statehood. Under the Timber Culture Act, the government promised to give land to anyone who planted trees on the prairie. By planting a token number of willows and oaks, the railroads gobbled up land that they then rented or sold at inflated prices. Eventually, the railroads owned almost one-fourth of North Dakota. It was as if the prairie wind blew bushels of cash directly into the railroads' bank accounts.

Empty land wasn't profitable for the railroads, however. They needed a population of farmers and city folk who depended on rail travel. Representatives of the rail lines went as far afield as Europe to attract settlers. Of course, the promoters neglected to mention North Dakota's harsh winters, locusts, droughts, and floods. Advertisements in hundreds of newspapers played up the rich, easily cultivated soil.

Opposite: A farmer
looking for rain

Threshing wheat

Immigrants

Immigrants poured into North American ports from Norway, Sweden, Denmark, Germany, and Switzerland, among many other countries. All were ready to make a new world for themselves and their families. Most landed in the Great Lakes ports of Superior, Duluth, Green Bay, Milwaukee, Kenosha, and Chicago.

From there, they moved inland by train, much to the rail lines' delight. Freight cars hauled all the essentials necessary to set up farming on the plains, including mowers, reapers, cultivators, seeders, horses, cattle, barrels of nails, coils of rope, pot-bellied stoves, and boxes of hammers. Passenger coaches packed with excited newcomers paused only briefly in Bismarck and the state's other cities to unload their human cargo. These immigrant trains helped boost the population of the young state. In 1900, the state's population hit 319,000, and it reached 577,000 only a decade later.

A Future President in North Dakota

In the 1880s, the future president Theodore Roosevelt was one of those staking a claim in North Dakota. He farmed and raised cattle at Elkhorn Ranch along the Little Missouri River in the Badlands. He learned to appreciate the beauty of the unforgiving land and became a strong supporter of environmental issues. He returned to western North Dakota often over the years to hunt and enjoy the landscape. During a visit to Fargo in 1910, Roosevelt said, "If it had not been for what I learned during those years that I spent here in North Dakota, I never in the world would have been president of the United States." ■

New Government and New Governors

On the day statehood was declared, farmer and land speculator John Miller took office as the first governor. The state's assembly met on November 19, 1889, only seventeen days after President Benjamin Harrison signed the state into existence. Legislators worked hard to pass laws to rein in the most obvious abuses of the railroads and grain firms. They also drew up plans for a much-needed system of county and city governments. Ordinary North Dakotans felt that things were finally in their favor.

Yet living on the frontier was still tough. Hundreds of orphans from the big cities in the East were sent to North Dakota to work as farm laborers in exchange for room and board. Brothers and sisters were often separated when the trains unloaded, never to see each other again. Although most farmers were kind, some were cruel and uncaring, considering the young workers nothing more than free labor. An orphan named Andrew Burke who had been sent to Indiana as a nine-year-old eventually made his way to North Dakota and became the second governor of the state—from 1891 to 1893.

A reform candidate and another governor named Burke—the tough-talking Irishman John Burke—was elected governor in 1906. He was so popular that he was reelected two more times.

John Burke was elected North Dakota governor in 1906.

Under his three administrations, laws were passed to protect farmers and workers. In direct primary elections, voters instead of powerful business groups selected candidates.

Governor John Burke worked hard to curb child-labor abuses. After serving as governor, he was appointed treasurer of the United States and named chief justice of North Dakota's supreme court. Burke is memorialized by a statue in the Capitol in Washington, D.C. He is the only North Dakotan so honored, although a second statue honoring Sacajawea is planned.

Farm Cooperatives

But the farmers still had problems. The grain companies and railroads conspired to pay little for crops and charge high rates for shipping the flood of corn and wheat from the Great Plains states. Often, it seemed like the government was on the side of big business, at the expense of the ordinary citizen. Even the U.S. Supreme Court usually ruled in favor of corporations when it came to interstate commerce and contract issues.

Finally, the farmers had enough. They formed cooperatives, banding together to buy seed and equipment and sell their agricultural products. In this way, they negotiated better deals and relieved some of their economic burden.

After the Civil War (1861–1865) and well into the early twentieth century, farmers' organizations voiced the concerns of farmers. These groups included the Grange, the Greenback Party, the Farmers' Alliance, and the Populists.

These groups advocated "democratic agriculture," supporting the idea that elected officials should work for the voters instead of favoring big business. The rural community waged an uphill battle against the powerful urban corporations that controlled the storage, transportation, and milling of crops. One important success was the institution of a uniform system of weighing grain. Eventually, the determined farmers broke the domination of the Minneapolis grain merchants and the banks.

Arthur Townley and the Nonpartisan League

One North Dakotan farmer, Arthur Townley (above), formed the Nonpartisan League in 1915 after he lost his farm. A convincing speaker, he eventually encouraged 40,000 other angry farmers to join his political group. In 1918, the league's candidates held every state office but one. In 1919, the league helped set up the Bank of North Dakota in Bismarck to provide lower interest rates on loans to the state's farmers. ■

A Time of Growth

All this time, North Dakota continued to grow, driven by agriculture. Between 1890 and 1901, the number of North Dakota farms rose from 45,000 to 74,000. Acreage in production reached 28.4 million acres (11.5 million ha). Some 80 percent of the crops were wheat. At the turn of the century, a hardier variety of wheat called durum was imported from Russia. Flax and bromegrass were also profitable crops.

On May 8, 1914, the Cooperative Extension Service was created. Under the direction of the North Dakota Agricultural College, agents visited farms to offer advice on improving agriculture.

With the support of the farmers' organizations, Republican Lynn J. Frazier was elected governor in 1916. From 1917 to 1921, he led efforts to improve rural schools. Frazier also pushed to lower taxes on farm improvements. This was also a boom time for North Dakota farmers because huge amounts of grain were needed during World War I (1914–1918) to feed the troops in Europe. By the 1920s, North Dakota farmers were cultivating some 36 million acres (14.6 million ha).

In the early 1900s, farmers had trouble making payments and keeping their farms.

The Great Depression

But trouble loomed. In the 1920s, debt and falling crop prices brought North Dakota to its knees. In 1929, the United States was hit by the Great Depression, a worldwide economic disaster that closed banks and industries and forced farmers off their land. North Dakota's population plummeted as displaced families sought work elsewhere. Trying to help their neighbors, some farmers blocked auctions on foreclosed farms by making low bids. They also withheld crops from market, in an effort to raise prices that had fallen to only thirty-one cents a bushel for wheat. But by the 1930s, more than one-third of the state's farmers had abandoned their farms.

"Wild Bill" Langer

William Langer, a leader of the Nonpartisan League, built an imposing political machine during the depression. As governor from 1933 to 1934, the colorful Langer was nicknamed Wild Bill because of his antics in blocking grain shipments and intimidating officials who were trying to auction off farms.

Langer got into hot water when he was accused of soliciting illegal political contributions from federal workers. He was tried, convicted, and removed from office. But he was reelected in 1936 as an independent, after his felony conviction was reversed. He became a U.S. senator in 1940 and died in office in 1959. ▪

Adding to the misery, a drought engulfed the plains states. Wells dried up, crops shriveled, and livestock died. Topsoil blew away, leaving sand and rocks where there had once been fertile fields. The "Dirty Thirties" were a grim time for North Dakota. In 1934, the state had a higher proportion of its residents on relief than any other state. By 1936, half of all North Dakotans were on relief.

The New Deal in North Dakota

In 1932, Franklin D. Roosevelt was elected president. A Democrat, Roosevelt pushed through programs and polices for economic recovery and reform called the New Deal. Many of these programs helped the nation's farmers. Roosevelt's New Deal programs brought electricity to rural areas, raised crop prices, offered better loan terms, and provided relief payments.

The state allowed cooperatives to lease empty government land for grazing, which opened up thousands of acres to cattle. Soil conservation districts were established to enforce land-use regulations and the State Water Commission was formed to develop water-preservation strategies. Federal programs put unemployed

President Franklin D. Roosevelt (seated) signing a farm bill in 1933

North Dakotans to work building many of the state's roads, bridges, parks, and historic sites.

These programs, along with increased rainfall that produced bumper crops, helped North Dakota recover slowly in the 1940s. After 1941, when the United States entered World War II (1939–1945), the state's crops were once again in high demand. Many farmers were exempted from military service because their agricultural skills were needed. Thousands of other young North Dakotan men and women marched off to war.

In 1942, a lobbying group for farmers called the North Dakota Farm Bureau was set up. The farm bureau drew many members from the western part of the state. The North Dakota Farmers Union, a less conservative group founded in 1927, was also active. Both organizations made sure that North Dakota farmers had a voice on the political scene on state and national levels.

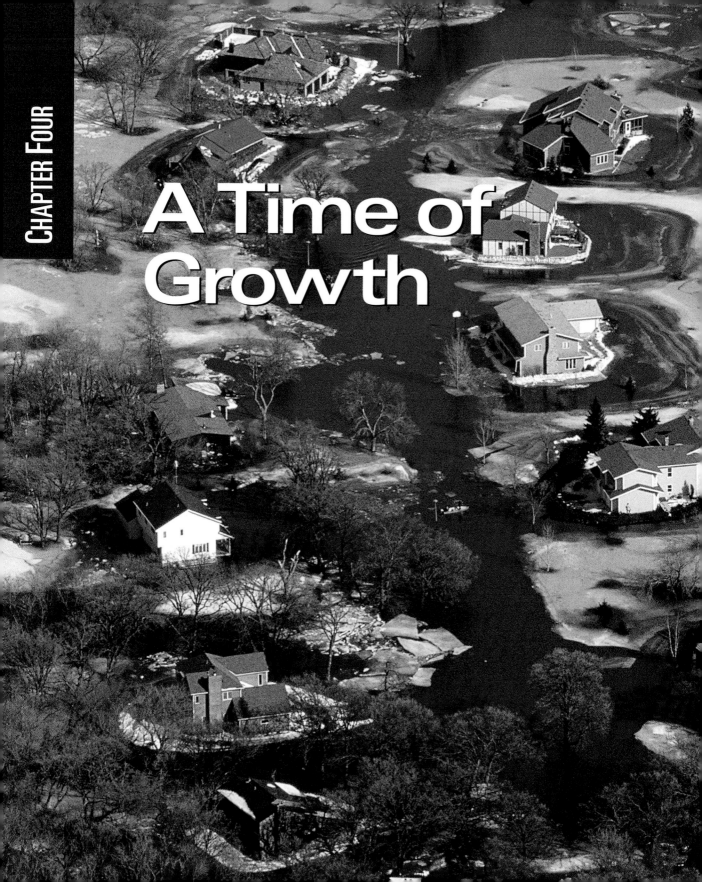

CHAPTER FOUR

A Time of Growth

Building Garrison Dam

t took years for North Dakota to fully recover from the Great Depression. In the 1940s, its population dropped. The state lost 22,000 residents between the late 1930s and 1940s. Despite this challenge, North Dakota struggled to rebuild itself. Young veterans returned from military service and went to school under the GI Bill, a government program that helped pay for college.

The Pick-Sloan Act, a federal development plan in the Missouri River basin, set the state's economy in motion. Under the plan, construction of Garrison Dam began in 1946. The towering dam, one of the largest earth-filled dams in the nation, was completed in 1960. The structure produced electricity, helped relieve flooding along the river, and provided irrigation water, while its backwaters created Lake Sakakawea, a favorite fishing and boating reservoir.

Opposite: Spring flooding in Fargo

Unfortunately, the project also flooded farms, ranches, businesses, and Indian reservation lands. All of them now lie under the waters of Lake Sakakawea.

Improving Roads

Since so many North Dakotans live in remote rural areas, transporting crops, livestock, and goods to market has always been a concern. Although railroads were still an important part of the state's transportation system, advances in motorized transportation and the improvement of roads in the early twentieth century had already made their mark. In 1904, North Dakota had 59,000 miles (94,931 km) of roads. Unfortunately, they were mostly dirt roads that turned to mud when it rained. Farmers often earned a few extra

Railroads have always been important to North Dakota.

dollars pulling vehicles out of the muck with their horses. In those days, only 200 miles (322 km) of the state's roads were gravel.

The Federal Aid Road Act of 1916 provided money to the states for improving their roads. North Dakota eagerly took advantage, building 4,300 miles (6,919 km) of new roads by 1930. To the relief of motorists, 2,800 miles (4,505 km) were gravel and a few were made of asphalt. However, the longest stretch of concrete was only 7 miles (11 km).

The trucking of livestock was in its infancy in the 1930s, but by 1940, more concrete highways and better trucks changed the way North Dakotans shipped goods. Most livestock was shipped by rail to the meat packers at the beginning of the century. Only forty years later, more than 60 percent of all sheep and cattle sent to the processing plants in West Bismarck were sent by truck.

In the 1950s, construction began on the interstate highway system, which was completed in 1977. Today, most processed goods move by truck, while more than 70 percent of all grain shipments are still made by rail.

Changes in Farming

Mechanization of agriculture was also increasing by the 1950s. North Dakota had more tractors and other motorized farm implements than any other state, but its farmers still had a tough time. When they used pesticides and chemical fertilizers to increase yields, prices dropped because too many crops were harvested.

To help alleviate the problem of oversupply in the 1960s, the federal government launched the Soil Bank project. Under this plan, farmers were paid to *not* plant seeds for a time. It

In the 1950s, farm equipment became more mechanized.

helped level the crop-pricing hurdle and allowed the land to recover. Eventually, nearly 10 percent of North Dakota's fertile cropland found its way into the Soil Bank. Following this plan, Congress then approved the Conservation Reserve Program, which deliberately idled thousands of acres in North Dakota in the 1980s.

The roller-coaster farm situation continued into the 1970s. In 1971, farmers were lucky to get $1.70 for a bushel of wheat. It was a difficult time for many farmers, who knew no other way of life. One North Dakotan farmer lamented, "If I won $1 million in the lottery, I'd keep farming until the money was all gone!" The next year, prices soared when additional grain was shipped to the Soviet Union, which had suffered a bad harvest.

In 1972, sugar-beet growers in North Dakota and Minnesota purchased the American Crystal Sugar plant in Moorhead. They formed the Minn-Dak Farmers Cooperative, the first farmer-owned

An aerial view of the Minn-Dak Farmers Cooperative

beet-processing cooperative in the state. In another step to help the struggling family farmer in the 1980s, the state passed legislation that allowed family corporations to own farms.

Times remained tough for North Dakota's farmers well into the 1990s. Canadian imports of wheat and barley flooded American markets after the passage of the 1994 North American Free Trade Agreement (NAFTA), which made Canada, Mexico, and the United States one of the world's largest free-trade zones. Angry farmers protested at crossing points along the Canada–United States border, but the movement of grain continued.

Faced with such competition, there was an even greater need to diversify the state's agricultural and business economy. A number of ranchers took up buffalo raising. The North American Bison Cooperative set up a federally approved slaughterhouse in New Rockford, and a company called Avikko built a potato-processing plant at Jamestown. Other firms moved into niche areas that helped

Sunflowers

Bright, cheery sunflowers have been grown as a snack food in North Dakota for a long time. In the 1960s, doors to a new market swung open. In the former Soviet Union, sunflower oil was used often for cooking. The people there needed North Dakota sunflower products. Sunflowers became known as Russian peanuts, and North Dakota, once known mostly for its wheat, earned additional fame for its sunflowers. Sunflower-processing plants now operate in West Fargo, Enderlin, and Velva. ▪

the agricultural sector. For instance, ProGold built a $260 million corn-sweetener plant at Wahpeton.

Future Challenges

North Dakotans would like to forget the winter of 1996 and 1997. The weather was exceptionally difficult. Deep snow and lots of rain

contributed to widespread flooding that heavily damaged the city of Grand Forks and other communities along the Missouri, the Red River of the North, and their tributaries. The high water drowned livestock and flooded fields. As the water receded, fungus destroyed acres of vegetation. However, by the end of the 1990s, Grand Forks had slowly come back to life and the fields were dry again.

As North Dakota moves into the next century, its people face many of the same difficulties as its original settlers. The state remains rural and dependent on an agricultural, commodity-based economy. The lack of a large population base prevents an expansion of industry. The computer age and technology may offer a bridge to the rest of the world that geography and climate have prohibited until now.

April 1997 flooding caused damage to Fargo and other communities.

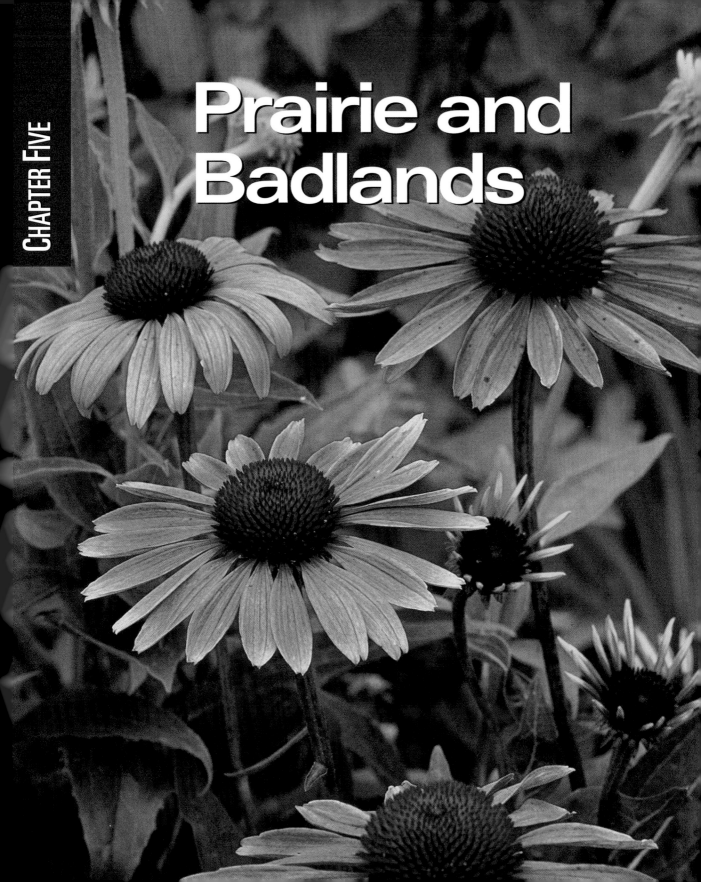

Chapter Five

Prairie and Badlands

North Dakota has a marvelous variety of natural wonders. From its purple coneflowers and its nighttime canopy of stars over the Badlands to its aspen and oak leaves changing their seasonal colors, North Dakota offers much more than a flat expanse of fertile farmland.

Geological Origins

Long after its fiery beginning, Earth eventually cooled. It became so cold that great masses of ice moved out from the North Pole. These sheets of ice were glaciers. Some were several miles high, making their way down from what is now Canada. They retreated, returned, and retreated again at least a dozen times. Every visit changed the landscape—rock was layered upon rock. Some formations were ground down or flattened and new ones were created.

Geologists, scientists who study rocks, have named the four epochs, or periods of time, during which the land that is now North Dakota was formed. Geologists dig far down through Earth's crust to find the rock making up these ages.

Morning light over the Badlands

Opposite: Purple coneflowers

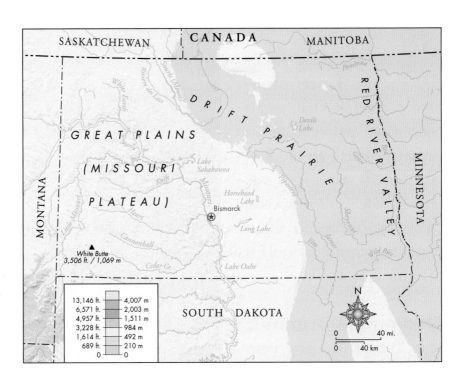

North Dakota's topography

The first was the Cryptozoic age, which provided the hard underpinning of North Dakota's landscape. Next was the Paleozoic age, which covered the first rocks with many layers of sandstone, shale, and limestone. Extensive oil deposits are found in this layer. Then came the Mesozoic age, complete with dinosaurs that splashed happily in a great sea that probably stretched from the Arctic Circle to the Gulf of Mexico. Fossils from these centuries litter the western part of the state. The Cenozoic age was the last of the major eras. In this era, vast beds of brown-black lignite (coal) were formed from decayed vegetation. They are now mined.

Around 13,000 years ago, ice sheets and huge mounds of glacial rubble blocked the northward-flowing Red River of the North and created the vast Lake Agassiz. When the lake eventually drained, its wide flat bed formed the fertile Red River valley, which stretches from North Dakota into Canada along the border of Minnesota. The valley is the lowest point in North Dakota, at 750 feet (229 meters) above sea level. The glaciers also pushed the Missouri River and other waterways into the banks we see today.

The Land

North Dakota has a total area of 70,704 square miles (183,123 square kilometers). About 2 percent of this, or 1,710 square miles (4,429 sq km), is water. The state is 310 miles (499 km) wide at the Canadian border on the north and 360 miles (579 km) wide on its boundary with South Dakota. It stretches 210 miles (338 km) from north to south.

North Dakota has three distinct land areas: the Red River valley, the drift prairie, and the Great Plains. The Red River valley is one of the best farming regions in the world, with fertile soil several feet thick. It is also the most populous part of the state.

The drift prairie lies along the western side of the Red River valley, several hundred feet higher than the valley floor. A sheer slope called an escarpment marks the boundary between the two land formations. Here, glaciers dumped millions of tons of drift—a finely ground, powderlike soil that is wonderfully fertile for growing crops. This region is noted for its rolling hills, lakes, and streams. In the north, the Turtle Mountains rise some 550 feet (168 m) above the landscape. These heavily wooded hills, near Canada, encompass an area about 25 miles (40 km) from north to south and 44 miles (71 km) from east to west.

Farmland in the Turtle Mountains

The Great Plains cover the southwestern half of the state, running from Canada all the way to Texas. In North Dakota, this part of the plains is called the Missouri Plateau. It rises to a slope about 300 to 400 feet (92 to 122 m) upwards from the drift prairie east of the Missouri River. Many of the state's mineral deposits are hidden here under the surface. Herds of white-faced Herefords and other cattle graze on this landscape. White Butte in Slope County is the highest location in North Dakota, towering 3,506 feet (1,069 m) above sea level.

The Badlands

The Dakota Badlands begin along the Little Missouri River. These land formations were called *mauvaises terres á traverser*, or "bad lands to travel through," by the first French explorers.

Erosion from the river began carving the landscape 600,000 to 700,000 years ago. The water action created clay hummocks, sandstone hills, and rock formations. A 600-foot (183-m)-deep canyon in the heart of the Badlands slices through the rock. Some of the lignite found there has been burning for hundreds of years, with its intense heat creating rough fragments of crustlike lava called scoria.

The Little Missouri River runs through the Dakota Badlands.

Water

North Dakota has large quantities of above- and below-surface water. The state's major lakes and reservoirs encompass nearly 863,000 acres (349,515 ha). The main rivers and their tributaries meander across 5,100 miles (8,206 km).

The Missouri River is North Dakota's largest source of water.

Much of its flow comes from melting snow in its headwaters in western Montana and Wyoming. Except for the Missouri, the Red River, and lower stretches of the Sheyenne River, the state's streams often go dry during droughts. North Dakota's only large natural body of water is Devils Lake in the northeast.

Climate

North Dakota's climate is like that of the surrounding states in the upper Midwest, with plentiful sunshine, rain, and snow. Temperatures change regularly as the cold, dry air from the North Pole sweeps down to meet the warm, moist air from the south. North Dakotans are used to rapid switches in weather. Temperatures of 100° Fahrenheit (38° Celsius) or higher occur for a day or two in the summer every year. In the winter, temperatures can get as low as –40°F (–40°C).

North Dakota's Geographical Features

Total area; rank	70,704 sq. mi. (183,123 sq km); 18th
Land; rank	68,994 sq. mi. (178,694 sq km); 17th
Water; rank	1,710 sq. mi. (4,429 sq km); 18th
Inland water; rank	1,710 sq. mi. (4,429 sq km); 12th
Geographic center	Sheridan, 5 miles (8 km) southwest of McClusky
Highest point	White Butte, 3,506 feet (1,069 m)
Lowest point	At Red River, in Pembina County, 750 feet (229 m)
Largest city	Fargo
Population; rank	641,364 (1990 census); 47th
Record high temperature	121°F (49°C) at Steele on July 6, 1936
Record low temperature	–60°F (–51°C) at Parshall on February 15, 1936
Average July temperature	70°F (21°C)
Average January temperature	7°F (–14°C)
Average annual precipitation	17 inches (43 cm)

The first frosts occur around mid-September. January is the coldest month, with an average temperature of 7°F (–14°C). Some hearty North Dakotans sport bumper stickers that read –40°F KEEPS THE RIFFRAFF OUT.

Everyone is glad when April arrives. July is the warmest month, with an average temperature of 70°F (21°C). The highest temperature ever recorded in North Dakota was 121°F (49°C) at Steele, on July 6, 1936. The state's lowest temperature was –60° F (–51°C), recorded at Parshall on February 15, 1936.

Snow along the Red River

Precipitation

Annual snowfall in North Dakota ranges from less than 26 inches (66 centimeters) in Mountrail and McLean Counties to 38 inches (96 cm) from the northeast corner to the southwest. Many other states, including Arizona, New Mexico, and California, average more snow. However, in the winter of 1996 and 1997, Fargo was covered with a record 117 inches (297 cm) of snow. In January 1997, President Bill Clinton declared all fifty-three North Dakota counties disaster areas.

Rainfall in North Dakota peaks in June. The state has little rain in the autumn.

Opposite: North Dakota's snowfall brings days of sledding and skiing.

A rainy day in Bismarck

Grasslands

The state's grasslands are consistent from border to border. Western wheatgrass and thickspice wheatgrass are two of the most common grasses. Other varieties have such interesting names as needle-and-thread and porcupine grass. Blue grama grass can be found everywhere. Some 80 percent of North Dakota's pasturelands is made up of combinations of these grasses.

The Little Missouri National Grasslands covers more than 1 million acres (405,000 ha) of prairie and badlands. It is the largest and most diverse of twenty preserves located in eleven western states. For bikers and hikers, the 120-mile (193-km) Maad Daah Hey Trail—*Maad Daah Hey* means "grandfather" in Mandan—traverses the grasslands.

The Sheyenne National Grassland and the Cedar River Grassland are two other mixed-grass prairies in North Dakota for photographers, bird-watchers, horseback riders, and campers to enjoy. The Cedar River site, once a prime hunting land for Native Americans, also has a rich history. During one of General George Armstrong Custer's military forays into the region, his Seventh Cavalry troopers dug the symbol "US 7" into one of the hillsides. The marking is still there.

A Land of Few Forests

North Dakota has fewer forested areas than any other state. Only about 1 percent of the region has thick groves of trees, mostly along the banks of rivers and streams and in the Turtle Mountains. Basswood, box elder, ash, burr oak, white birch, and elms can be found

Opposite: The Sheyenne National Grassland

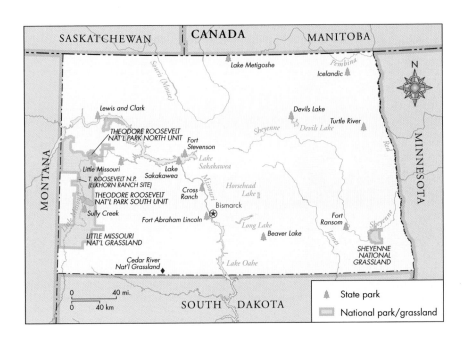

North Dakota's parks and forests

in eastern North Dakota. Cottonwood is common in the west, along with stands of yellow pine. Red cedar grows well in the Badlands. Farmers plant many varieties along the edges of their property to cut the strong winds.

Animals of the Region

Once abundant in the region's ancient lakes, a long-jawed crocodile-like creature is now just a stone-bound fossil. The remains of this monster, the world's only *Champsosaurus gigas*, are on exhibit in the North Dakota Heritage Center in Bismarck. A skeleton of an elephant-like mastodon, which once roamed the area's ancient grasslands, is also on display.

Today, the state's largest wild animals are bighorn sheep, whitetail and mule deer, antelope, and moose. Birds of all kinds live in

Bighorn sheep are among North Dakota's larger animals.

Theodore Roosevelt National Park

In 1908, President Theodore Roosevelt established the Dakota National Forest in Billings County. Until 1917, the land was under the administration of the Sioux National Forest. In 1998, it became part of the national grasslands system. The rugged Theodore Roosevelt National Park (above) covers about 70,000 acres (28,350 ha) along the Missouri River as a memorial to the twenty-sixth president. This park was established in 1947 as a national monument and was made a national park in 1978. ▪

Wild turkeys can be found throughout the state.

the state year-round and flock there during migration season. North Dakota is the number-one producer of waterfowl in the continental United States. Sharptail and sage grouse, wild turkeys, Canada geese, and numerous species of ducks are found here. The Hungarian partridge, an excellent game bird and a favorite of upland hunters, was introduced into North Dakota in 1923.

North Dakota instituted the Waterfowl Management Plan in 1986 when state residents began to realize that drought and other

conditions—both natural and man-made—were affecting the bird population. By the summer of 1993, as the state's wetlands filled again with plenty of rain and melting snow, the birds had returned in greater numbers.

Fishing fans love casting for catfish, salmon, bullhead, rainbow trout, bass, northern pike, yellow perch, and walleye pike in rivers and man-made reservoirs such as Sakakawea, Oahe, Ashtabula, and Bowman-Haley. Federal fish hatcheries at Riverdale and Valley City help manage the state's fish reserves.

North Dakota's landscape has much to offer.

CHAPTER SIX

Cities with a Frontier Heritage

orth Dakota's cities reflect their frontier heritage. Many communities originated as fur-trading posts or army forts. Others trace their heritage to Native American encampments.

Bismarck

Bismarck, the state capital, is in the lower central half of North Dakota. First called Edwinton, the village grew until it became the capital of Dakota Territory in 1883 after Yankton, South Dakota. When North Dakota became a state in 1889, the city remained the capital.

Gold prospectors and soldiers used the Bismarck area as a jumping-off point for their adventures. Among the first were explorers Meriwether Lewis and William Clark, who camped not far from today's Bismarck in 1804. General George Armstrong Custer was commander of nearby Fort Abraham Lincoln, and his men often visited Bismarck when off duty in the early 1870s.

A view of Bismarck

Opposite: North Dakotans reenact a cavalry charge at Fort Abraham Lincoln.

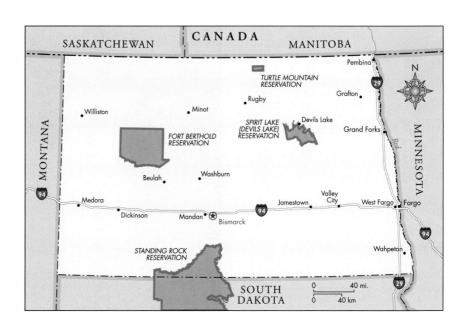

North Dakota's cities and interstates

One of the best places to discover North Dakota's rich Native American heritage is at the North Dakota Heritage Center, headquarters of the State Historical Society of North Dakota, on the capitol grounds. Visitors can travel the corridors of time from the First People exhibit with an authentic tepee and examples of clothing, tools, and pottery, through exploration, settlement, and pre–World War II eras. Also on display are artifacts from Sitting Bull, Theodore Roosevelt, and North Dakota's astronauts.

In addition, Bismarck continues to be the commercial hub of North Dakota and the center of the state's rail and highway system. In the 1940s, the city was the headquarters for the Garrison Engineer District, which was responsible for building the Garrison Dam.

When the capitol burned in 1930, some legislators wanted to move the state government to another city. However, a popular vote

kept Bismarck as the state's governmental seat. A new capitol was constructed between 1933 and 1935. The simple nineteen-story structure with interior designs of marble and hardwood was fronted with white Indiana limestone. The entire building cost only $2 million, a fact appreciated by North Dakotans at the height of the Great Depression. It is a fine example of a graceful architectural design called art deco.

The capitol's exterior is made of limestone.

A Historic Fort

Fort Abraham Lincoln was built in 1872 near a Mandan village called On-A-Slant. The military post once housed 1,000 men. One colorful character at the fort was Isaiah Dorman, an African-American who married a Sioux woman. Because he could speak several Native American dialects, he rode alongside the cavalry's Arikara scouts far out ahead of the main troops.

The complex holds General George Armstrong Custer's rebuilt house (above) as well as barracks and other buildings. In 1876, Custer marched out from the fort on his way into Montana Territory where Native Americans eventually killed him and about 210 of his men at the Battle of Little Bighorn. Visitors can see the fort from an observation tower at the state capitol in Bismarck.

The fort became North Dakota's first state park in 1907. Cannon firings, cavalry charges, and infantry drills are held there regularly during the summer. ■

Jamestown

Jamestown, midway between Bismarck and Fargo, started as a typical railroad town in the 1870s. The earliest settlers were workers for the Northern Pacific Railway, followed by farmers whose fields lay in the James River valley. Fort Seward was built in 1872 to protect the growing village. The world's largest buffalo statue stands at the edge of town as a monument to the great herds that once roamed here.

One of the most impressive railroad bridges in the United States is in nearby Valley City. Opened in 1905 and still in operation, the High Line Bridge spans the Sheyenne River. The bridge is 3,338 feet (1,018 m) long and rises 126 feet (38 m) above the riverbed.

Fargo

Fargo, incorporated in 1875, is the largest city in North Dakota. It has 74,111 residents, according to the 1990 census. The city is located directly across the Red River of the North from Moorhead, Minnesota. Fargo, the county seat of Cass County, is in the heart of the Red River valley wheat country. It was named for William Fargo, a director of the Northern Pacific Railway and cofounder of American Express and Wells Fargo Express. During planting and harvesting seasons, the area's fields are full of giant tractors that look like huge iron bugs. Fargo's farmers call their county the Bread Basket of the World.

The city of Fargo has a strong industrial sector, especially in computer software development. Local companies also make concrete, metal products, and electrical components. Fargo's

Bonanzaville, USA, in Fargo

Bonanzaville, USA, Museum is a sprawling site containing forty frontier buildings from the turn of the century. One of the homes belonged to David H. Houston, the inventor of photographic roll film—one of the first products made by the Eastman Kodak Company.

Grand Forks

Grand Forks, where the Red River of the North merges with the Red Lake River, lies 73 miles (117 km) north of Fargo. Several homes here hearken back to the city's days as a frontier outpost. One of them is the 1879 home of Tom Campbell, a farmer whose management of thousands of acres of land in North Dakota earned him the nickname the Wheat King.

The city remains an agricultural hub, with nearby fields bursting with wheat, sugar beets, corn, barley, flax, potatoes, and oats. Herds of cattle graze on pastures at the outskirts of its suburbs. Grand Forks was founded in 1871 and incorporated in 1881.

Oldest Log Cabin

A cabin built in 1843 at Walhalla is North Dakota's oldest existing building. A trader named Norman Kittson built the little log house. ■

Red River Floods

On Friday, April 18, 1997, the Red River of the North poured over the dikes into the Lincoln Drive neighborhood of Grand Forks. By Saturday night, floodwaters had spread over large areas of Grand Forks and the adjacent town of East Grand Forks, Minnesota. More than 60,000 people—almost the entire population of the two cities—were forced from their homes. Eleven buildings on three downtown blocks, includ-ing the offices of the *Grand Forks Herald* newspaper, were damaged or destroyed in fires because fire trucks could not get close enough to put out the flames. The *Herald* never missed a day of publication though. After the flood, thousands of volunteers from around the country helped in the cleanup. The paper won a Pulitzer Prize for its effort in reporting during and after the flood. ■

Selkirkers

Encouraged by Scotsman Thomas Douglas, the Earl of Selkirk, a band of hardy Scots and Irish peasants received permission from the Hudson's Bay Company to farm land near Fort Douglas. The fort was in Canadian territory along the Red River of the North. The "Selkirkers" were supposed to grow food for the Hudson's Bay workers in nearby trading posts.

At the beginning, the new arrivals had neither seeds nor farm equipment, so they almost starved. They survived their first winter by eating buffalo meat. Compounding the problem, rival traders from other companies resented their presence, believing that farming would cut into their business.

After a short time, the community moved into the Pembina area of North Dakota. But in 1816, a bloody fight broke out between the trappers and the farmers. Twenty Selkirkers were killed in what they called the Massacre of Seven Oaks.

In 1818, Father Sévère Dumolin built a Catholic chapel at Pembina, just in time for the community to pray for the end of a plague of locusts. In 1818, a survey showed that the settlement was in U.S. territory, but most of the surviving Selkirkers had already gone back to Canada. ■

Pembina

In the far northeastern corner of North Dakota, Pembina sits on the Canadian border where the Pembina River joins the Red River of the North. The name *Pembina* comes from the Cree Indian word meaning "high-bush cranberry." The city's heritage stretches far back into frontier history. Trappers and traders from the North West, the XY, and Hudson's Bay Companies built rival posts in the vicinity in the eighteenth and early nineteenth centuries.

Fort Totten State Historic Site

In east-central North Dakota on the south shore of Devils Lake, the Fort Totten State Historic Site (above), is the best-preserved military garrison on the Great Plains. General Alfred Totten established the fort in 1867 to protect overland freight lines from Minnesota to western Montana. After the fort was decommissioned in 1890, the post went through several changes. First, it became a boarding school for Native American youngsters, then it was a tuberculosis hospital, and eventually it served as a reservation school. While many of the other forts of the era were built of wood, Fort Totten's barracks, storehouses, and other structures were made of clay bricks. ◼

Minot

Minot, in far north-central North Dakota, was settled in 1886 and incorporated in 1887. Farmers have long hauled their crops to Minot for shipping by rail.

The town of Minot dates back to 1886.

The U.S. military has had a presence in Minot since the days of the Indian wars. Activated in 1957, the sprawling Minot Air Force Base is 13 miles (21 km) north of the city. It covers 5,000 acres (2,020 ha), with runways and hangars serving the Fifth Bomb Wing and its giant B-52 bombers. The Ninety-First Missile Wing supervises a Minuteman III missile complex that spreads across another 8,000 square miles (20,720 sq km) of surrounding public land. The base is one of the largest employers in the state with 6,300 military and civilian workers.

Washburn, Hazen, and Beulah

Lake Sakakawea and a cluster of ancient Native American sites lie southwest of Minot, near where the Knife and Missouri Rivers merge. The present-day towns of Washburn and Hazen stand where Arikara, Hidatsa, and Mandan villages once thrived. The region's Cross Ranch State Park and Cross Ranch Nature Preserve

Jane Kurtz and Flood Poems

While participating in a program led by local children's author Jane Kurtz (above), many children from Grand Forks wrote poems and stories about their experiences during the great flood. Kurtz's own collection of poems about the flood, *River Friendly, River Wild*, was published in 2000. She helped the children voice their feelings and concerns about the floods. Here is a poem by a fifth-grade student named Lacey Kallinen:

The Big, Big Flood
I touched my dog Gabby.
She felt soggy.
I heard sirens, and they sounded
like screaming.
I saw people crying. It looked like
broken hearts.
It looked like rain falling down
their faces.
The muck and old fish smelled
bad.
I tasted Red Cross food. It tasted
like junk.
A pontoon came lolloping in the
waves into my yard. ■

include the last 7 free-flowing miles (11 km) of the once unharnessed Missouri River.

Beulah, in Mercer County, was the site of French explorer Charles Le Raye's camp in the early 1800s. The Brulé Sioux captured Le Raye. As a prisoner of the tribe, he was one of the first whites to see the Rocky Mountains. When he was released, his descriptions of the Knife River encouraged other explorations deep into what would become west-central North Dakota.

Medora

In the far west, Medora lies near the Little Missouri River in the center of the North Dakota Badlands. A military outpost was established there in 1879 to protect railroad workers. It evolved into a robust cattle town and a transport center for shipping beef to market. The Rough Riders Hotel in Medora lent its name to the famous

Medora is home to the Rough Riders Hotel.

The Marquis de Mores

The Marquis de Mores, a French speculator, wanted to open a packing plant in Medora with his father-in-law's money. He planned to slaughter range-fed cattle and ship the dressed meat in refrigerated railcars to eastern markets. The concept was good, but competition from big packing cities such as Chicago and a preference of buyers for corn-fed beef put him out of business in 1886. The marquis and his wife, Medora, headed off to more adventures in North Africa, where he was killed. All that remains of his plant is a brick smokestack and a foundation. A statue of the marquis (right) stands in the town's De Mores Memorial Park. The twenty-six-room house he built for his family's summer visits to Medora is preserved today as the Chateau de Mores State Historic Site. ■

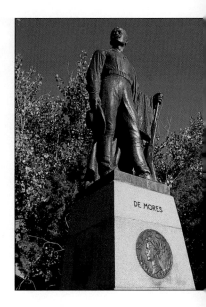

cavalry unit led by Theodore Roosevelt in Cuba during the Spanish-American War. The town was named for Medora von Hoffman Vallambrosa, the American wife of the Marquis de Mores, a French entrepreneur.

CHAPTER SEVEN

Serving the People

North Dakota's capitol grounds

like the other states in the Union, North Dakota has executive, legislative, and judicial branches of government. Each branch works to protect the rights of North Dakotans and represents their interests.

Executive Branch

The governor, the chief elected officer of the state, heads the executive branch. The governor serves for four years. He or she must be a U.S. citizen, at least thirty years old, and a resident of North Dakota for five years before the election. These requirements ensure that every candidate knows the state and how it operates.

Opposite: Inside the house of representatives

North Dakota's Governors

Name	Party	Term	Name	Party	Term
John Miller	Rep.	1889–1891	George F. Shafer	Rep.	1929–1933
Andrew H. Burke	Rep.	1891–1893	William Langer	Rep.	1933–1934
Eli C. D. Shortridge	Ind.	1893–1895	Ole H. Olson	Rep.	1934–1935
Roger Allin	Rep.	1895–1897	Thomas H. Moodie	Dem.	1935
Frank A. Briggs	Rep.	1897–1898	Walter Welford	Rep.	1935–1937
Joseph M. Devine	Rep.	1898–1899	William Langer	Rep.	1937–1939
Frederick B. Fancher	Rep.	1899–1901	John Moses	Dem.	1939–1945
Frank White	Rep.	1901–1905	Fred G. Aandahl	Rep.	1945–1951
E. Y. Sarles	Rep.	1905–1907	C. Norman Brunsdale	Rep.	1951–1957
John Burke	Dem.	1907–1913	John E. Davis	Rep.	1957–1961
L. B. Hanna	Rep.	1913–1917	William L. Guy	Dem.	1961–1973
Lynn J. Frazier	Rep.	1917–1921	Arthur A. Link	Dem.	1973–1981
R. A. Nestos	Rep.	1921–1925	Allen I. Olson	Rep.	1981–1985
A. G. Sorlie	Rep.	1925–1928	George A. Sinner	Dem.	1985–1992
Walter Maddock	Rep.	1928–1929	Edward T. Schafer	Rep.	1992–

Governor Ed Schafer took office in 1992.

The governor, the commissioner of agriculture, and the attorney general exercise joint power through the Industrial Commission. The old Nonpartisan League established this commission years ago to manage state-owned industries.

The governor has many duties, from serving as commander of North Dakota's National Guard to recommend-

North Dakota's State Government

Executive Branch

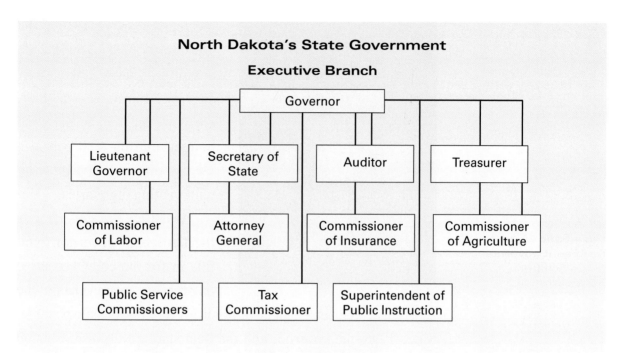

Governor			

Lieutenant Governor	Secretary of State	Auditor	Treasurer
Commissioner of Labor	Attorney General	Commissioner of Insurance	Commissioner of Agriculture

Public Service Commissioners	Tax Commissioner	Superintendent of Public Instruction

Legislative Branch

Senate	House of Representatives

Judicial Branch

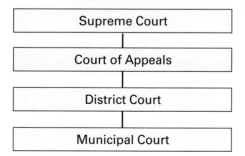

Supreme Court
Court of Appeals
District Court
Municipal Court

Rosemarie Myrdal, lieutenant governor in the Schafer administration

ing legislation. A day for the governor's office might include chairing a Devils Lake Advisory Committee meeting, checking an item in the state budget, cutting a ribbon at a factory opening, and meeting with visiting dignitaries.

Assisting the governor is the lieutenant governor, who fills in for the chief executive on occasion. As president of the state senate, the lieutenant governor has a very responsible position. Since 1996, the governor and the lieutenant governor have been elected on the same party ballot and voters cast one vote for both candidates.

Legislative Branch

The North Dakota legislative assembly is made up of the house and the senate. The legislature is the official caretaker of the state constitution. The legislative assembly represents the interests of the voters. It makes the laws and raises the money to pay for state government. The legislative assembly also approves the governor's appointees to the state board of higher education and the gaming commission.

To serve in the legislature, a North Dakota resident must be at least eighteen years old and have lived in the state at least a year

Pioneering Women Legislators

After the Nineteenth Amendment to the U.S. Constitution was passed in 1920, giving women the right to vote, Minnie Craig (above) of the Nonpartisan League and Nellie Dougherty, a Democrat, were the first women legislators elected in North Dakota. Craig and Dougherty were elected in 1922. Craig retired in 1934, after a session as speaker of the house. She was the first woman in the United States to serve as speaker of the house in a state legislature.

Brynhild Haugland of Minot was honored in 1989 as the longest-serving state legislator in the United States. When she retired in 1990, she had been in North Dakota's house of representatives since 1938 and cast an estimated 22,000 votes! Haugland was born in 1905 to Norwegian immigrants. Agnes Geelan, who had been mayor of Enderlin, became the state's first woman state senator when she was elected in 1950.

These pioneers paved the way for other women. By the 1970s, thirty-one women served in the legislature. In 1989, the state's centennial year, twenty-four women were elected. Through the 1980s, forty women were legislators including many young mothers. One of them, Tish Kelly, a Democrat from Fargo, became speaker of the house exactly fifty years after Minnie Craig served in that position.

By the end of the 1990s, forty-three women had served their state as legislators. In 1993, Rosemarie Myrdal, as lieutenant governor, became the second woman to serve as senate president. ▩

before the election. They start their term of office on the first day of December after the election. To ensure that the voters are equally represented, the legislative assembly reassigns the state's districts every ten years.

The legislature meets on the first Tuesday after the first Monday in January in odd-numbered years. It meets up to eighty days to conduct its business and can extend the time if necessary.

In the 1996 general election, voters increased the term of a

Keeping Up with the Times

North Dakota legislators are keeping up with the times. The legislative assembly has an Internet home page for information on legislators, committees, and the public (it is: *http://www.state.nd.us/lr/*). Since 1997, all legislators have received notebook computers. Now many senators and house members are enthusiastically using the computers to check on the status of bills, update their schedules, manage spreadsheets, and send e-mail messages. ■

State Flag and Seal

The state flag is similar to a regimental flag carried by the North Dakota Infantry in the Spanish-American War of 1898 and the Philippine Island insurrection in 1899. The flag was adopted on March 3, 1911.

The seal has undergone numerous design changes over the years, with the latest version approved in 1987. It features a tree in an open field; bundles of wheat, a plow, an anvil, and a sledge; a bow crossed with three arrows; and an Indian on horseback chasing a buffalo. The state logo, with forty-two stars and the date "October 1, 1889," the date the state constitution was approved, is also included. ■

North Dakota's State Symbols

State bird: Western meadowlark This yellow-breasted songbird (above) was adopted as the state bird on March 10, 1947.

State flower: Wild prairie rose This flower sports five pink petals with a cluster of yellow stamens in the center. The wild prairie rose grows alongside roads, in pastures, and in meadows. It was adopted as the state flower on March 7, 1907.

State fish: Northern pike This is one of the state's largest fish. The biggest northern pike ever caught in North Dakota waters was taken in Lake Sakakawea in 1968. It weighed 37 pounds 8 ounces (17 kg). The northern pike was adopted as the state fish on July 1, 1969.

State grass: Western wheatgrass This tough prairie grass once covered almost all of North Dakota. Western wheatgrass was adopted as the state grass on March 31, 1977.

State fossil: Teredo petrified wood A teredo is a worm-shaped mollusk related to clams and oysters. These so-called shipworms lived in the warm North Dakota swamps about 60 million years ago.

State tree: American elm This lovely tree often grows to heights of 120 feet (37 km) or taller. The American elm was adopted as the state tree on March 10, 1947.

State beverage: Milk The North Dakota legislature recognized the importance of the state's industry by making milk the official state beverage.

North Dakota's State Song
"North Dakota Hymn"

Words by James Foley   Music by C. S. Putnam

In 1926, Minnie J. Nielson, North Dakota superintendent of public instruction, asked poet James Foley of Bismarck to write the lyrics for a song about North Dakota. He created a poem that could be sung to the tune of "The Austrian Hymn." The first public performance of the "North Dakota Hymn" was in the Bismarck City Auditorium in 1927.

North Dakota, North Dakota,
With thy prairies wide and free,
All thy sons and daughter love
*   thee.*
Fairest state from sea to sea,
North Dakota, North Dakota,
Here we pledge ourselves to
*   thee.*
North Dakota, North Dakota,
Here we pledge ourselves to
*   thee.*

Hear thy loyal children singing,
Songs of happiness and
*   praise,*
Far and long the echoes ring-
*   ing*
Through the vastness of thy
*   ways—*
North Dakota, North Dakota,
We will serve thee all our days.
North Dakota, North Dakota,
We will serve thee all our days.

house member from two years to four years, the same length as a state senator's term. As a result of the vote, one-half of each chamber is elected every other year. The change took effect on July 1, 1997.

Judicial Branch

The judicial branch is made up of a state supreme court, district courts, and municipal courts as well as courts of appeals. Supreme court justices are elected for ten-year terms, district court judges are elected for six-year terms, and municipal judges have four-year terms. Judges do not belong to any political party.

North Dakota's supreme court has five judges. In 1999, the court had three male judges and two female judges. The highest court in North Dakota hears appeals from the lower courts. It also is responsible for maintaining high standards in the court system throughout the state. A temporary court of appeals was established in 1987 to assist the supreme court. Active or retired district court judges, retired supreme court justices, or appointed lawyers offer their expertise when the workload is heavy.

North Dakota's supreme court building

North Dakota's counties

Ronald Davies

Ronald Davies (1904–1996) was the federal jurist who ordered the integration of Little Rock Central High School in September 1957. His ruling in this Arkansas case allowed African-American youngsters to attend school with white students. Davies's scholarly interpretation of the law has been called a landmark decision on racial integration in the United States. Davies attended high school in Grand Forks, North Dakota, and graduated from the University of North Dakota in 1927. A lawyer, he served in the U.S. Army during World War II (1939–1945) and achieved the rank of lieutenant colonel. After the war, Davies continued his law practice in Grand Forks and was appointed a U.S. district judge in Fargo. He was named a senior district judge in 1971. ■

There are forty-seven district courts in North Dakota's fifty-three counties, divided into seven judicial districts. These courts supervise criminal and civil cases, as well as those involving juvenile offenders. The court also is responsible for the protection of children who are abandoned or abused.

There are also seventy-six municipal courts in the state. Most of their cases involve traffic charges.

On the Federal Level

On the federal level, North Dakota always has two senators who serve their state in Washington, D.C. The number of U.S. legisla-

Dr. Robert H. Bahmer

Dr. Robert H. Bahmer (1904–1990) was the fourth archivist of the United States, serving from 1966 to 1969 as head of the National Archives and Records Service. He also directed the presidential libraries of Presidents Herbert Hoover, Franklin D. Roosevelt, Harry S. Truman, and Dwight D. Eisenhower. ■

tors allowed for a state is based on its population. North Dakota had one representative from 1889 to 1902, two from 1903 to 1912, three from 1913 to 1932, two from 1933 to 1972, and one since 1973. This reflects the rise and fall of the state's population.

Chaplain for the U.S. Senate

Serving as chaplain for the U.S. Senate from 1981 until he retired in 1994, Reverend Richard C. Halverson (1916–1995) gave the daily prayer at the opening of each Senate session. Born in Pingree, North Dakota, he became a Presbyterian minister and headed a congregation in Maryland before going on to his chaplain duties in the Senate. Active in the International Prayer Breakfast movement, Halverson also spearheaded many social causes. He was a good friend of several presidents. Former president George Bush called him "one of God's very special messengers." He was named to North Dakota's Rough Rider Hall of Fame. ▪

CHAPTER EIGHT

A Farming Economy

A cattle ranch in the western part of the state

North Dakotans appreciate their abundance of valuable natural resources. Acres of crops and huge herds of grazing cattle cover the land, and generous reserves of gas and oil lie underneath it. The history of the state and the lives of its people are closely linked to the land.

Agriculture

Agriculture is the state's major business. North Dakota is one of the nation's leading wheat producers, ranking just after Kansas. It is first in the production of hard red spring wheat and durum. "Hard" refers to the high gluten content of the grain, which is important in bread making. Gluten is a sticky, healthful substance found in

Opposite: Harvesting wheat in central North Dakota

wheat flour. This wheat is often blended with softer wheats to increase the protein content of flour. Durum wheat, the hardest of all, is used in the production of pasta. North Dakota produces almost 75 percent of the durum in the United States.

North Dakota also leads the country in the production of barley. The state's farmers grew more than 100 million bushels in 1998, almost 30 percent of the nation's total. Barley is used for livestock feed and for making the malt used in brewing beer.

Barley is an important crop for North Dakota.

Oats are another cash crop for North Dakota farmers, who produce about 13 percent of the United States total. Oats are used

in cereal, bread, and horse feed. North Dakota also grows about 78 percent of the country's flax, an all-around grain used in manufacturing linseed oil, linen, and animal feed.

Other important crops provide the base for many manufactured products. Much of North Dakota's rye is used for making whiskey. The state is also a leading grower of sunflowers, which are used to make sunflower oil and snack foods. Potatoes, used for baking, chips, and french fries, are popular crops in the Red River valley. Corn, used as animal feed or for corn sweeteners, is grown in the southeastern corner of the state. In 1998, Cass County ranked number one in the production of the country's soybeans. The list continues with dry edible beans, canola, hay, field peas, buckwheat, lentils, and crambe, a crop used to produce machine lubricants.

Cass County is known for its production of soybeans.

North Dakotans get a big buzz out of their bees, consistently earning a place among the top three honey-producing states. Most of the state's beekeepers are migrants, however. They move their hives to warmer climates during the cold winters.

Livestock

Raising livestock is the economy's other agriculture business. Commercial feeder cattle are raised in every county. These calves

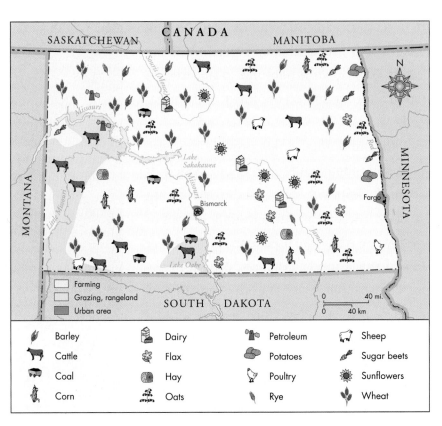

CANADA

SASKATCHEWAN   MANITOBA

MONTANA

MINNESOTA

Lake Sakakawea

Bismarck

Fargo

Lake Oahe

SOUTH   DAKOTA

☐ Farming
☐ Grazing, rangeland
■ Urban area

0 ——— 40 mi.
0 ——— 40 km

	Barley		Dairy		Petroleum		Sheep
	Cattle		Flax		Potatoes		Sugar beets
	Coal		Hay		Poultry		Sunflowers
	Corn		Oats		Rye		Wheat

North Dakota's natural resources

are weaned, or separated from their mothers, before being shipped to Nebraska, Iowa, Colorado, or Kansas for fattening and eventual slaughter. Among the most popular breeds are Angus, Hereford, Simmental, Charolais, and Saler.

The number of the state's dairy farms declined toward the end of the twentieth century, from about 1,750 in 1989 to 775 in 1999. However, ten bottling and processing plants in North Dakota still handle Grade A milk and other milk products. Feeder pigs remain big moneymakers in the southeastern counties where corn on the cob is plentiful. Pigs in the southwest corner of the

94 NORTH DAKOTA

state feed on barley, and some gourmets claim that pork chops from each side of the state taste deliciously unique as a result of this variety.

Although sheep, turkeys, and chickens are raised on some farms, North Dakota ranks only forty-fourth in the states for egg production. An increasing number of riding horses are bred in North Dakota. One interesting by-product of horse raising is the use of pregnant-mare urine as a basis for certain medications. Exotic animals such as bison, elk, llamas, emus, ostriches, and even cassowaries—large, flightless birds from Australia—are also found on North Dakota's farms.

Sheep are among the livestock raised in North Dakota.

Agricultural Organizations

The North Dakota commissioner of agriculture is responsible for overseeing the state's farming industry through the department of agriculture. The commissioner administers many programs to ensure that farmers are kept up-to-date on the latest growing techniques, environmental issues, and animal health and business practices. The department supports youth groups such as the 4-H and Future Farmers of America. Children show off their championship animals, vegetables, and crafts at county fairs and at the North Dakota State Fair held each year in Minot.

The state's universities take the lead in animal and crop

research, striving to make North Dakota's land as profitable and productive as possible. The North Dakota State University Agricultural Experiment Station in Fargo, chartered in 1890, and its eight research centers help state farmers. Additional state and federal departments also work to ensure only the finest products come out of North Dakota's farms. The state seed department certifies seed and specialty crops. And the National Resources Conservation Service works with private landowners to make sure their land is protected for their children's children.

Like their predecessors, North Dakota's farmers remain active in business and social organizations. The National Farmers Organization evolved from protests in the 1950s over low prices. It continues to be an important voice for the small farmer. The North Dakota Farm Bureau, founded in 1942, supports tax reform, groundwater protection, and health care for farm families. There are farm bureau chapters in every county. The North Dakota Farmers Union, formed in 1927, had 42,000 members in 1999. The union promotes cooperatives.

What North Dakota Grows, Manufactures, and Mines

Agriculture	Manufacturing	Mining
Barley	Food products	Clay
Beef cattle	Machinery	Coal
Milk		Limestone
Potatoes		Petroleum
Sugar beets		
Sunflower seeds		
Wheat		

There are many industry groups as well. North Dakota milk producers, barley growers, beekeepers, cattle breeders, and others all have groups that promote their members' interests.

The North Dakota State University Agricultural Experiment Station provides research that assists farmers throughout the state.

Energy Production

After agriculture, energy production is the most important segment of the state's economy. The economy is always affected by gas, oil, and coal prices. Fossil fuels such as lignite, a soft coal, are mined along the Missouri Slope. Lignite fuels many of the state's power

Fisherman's Catch Chowder

North Dakota's state fish is the northern pike, which tastes great in this hearty soup with another fish found in the state's waters— the rainbow trout.

Ingredients:

1 to 1 $\frac{1}{2}$ pounds pike and rainbow trout, combined

16 ounces whole tomatoes, fresh or canned, mashed

$\frac{1}{2}$ cup celery, chopped

$\frac{1}{2}$ cup onion, chopped

$\frac{1}{2}$ cup carrots, pared

$\frac{1}{4}$ cup parsley, snipped

1 teaspoon leaf rosemary

8 ounces clam juice

1 teaspoon salt

3 tablespoons flour

3 tablespoons butter or margarine, melted

$\frac{1}{3}$ cup light cream

Directions:

Clean the fish, then cut into 1-inch pieces.

In a two-quart crock pot, combine the fish and the rest of the ingredients except the flour, butter, and cream. Stir well. Cook on low setting for 7–8 hours, or on high setting for 3–4 hours.

One hour before serving, mix together butter, cream, and flour in a bowl. Stir the mixture into the crock pot and continue cooking until the mixture is slightly thickened.

Serves 4.

plants and is sold to customers around the world. Petroleum reserves can be found in the Williston Basin in northern and western North Dakota. Mandan has a large oil refinery.

Tourism

Tourism is a growing part of the state's economy today. Many visitors are drawn to North Dakota's historical sites. Forts, ancient Native American villages, pioneer homes, battlefields, and trail markers indicate where early North Dakotans lived and worked.

The North Dakota Parks and Recreation Department manages fifteen state parks and recreation areas around the state, totaling 19,271 acres (7,805 ha). By 1998, park visitors numbered more than 1 million annually. Ten of the parks are open year-round. Cross-country skiers love the Sheyenne River valley, and snowmobilers enjoy trails in the Turtle Mountains.

Cross-country skiing is a favorite of tourists and locals alike.

The International Peace Garden

The International Peace Garden (above) straddles North Dakota's border with the border of the Canadian province of Manitoba. The garden covers 2,339 acres (947 ha) of flowers, sculptures, and pavilions. It was dedicated in 1932, marking the long-standing peace between the United States and Canada.

An annual summer music camp attracts more than 2,000 young musicians. The Old-Time Fiddlers Contest and International Festival of the Arts draw thousands of listeners each summer. And every year, coaches from the United States and Canada run a camp to help young athletes hone their track-and-field skills. ■

Service Industries

The service industry contributes a large part of North Dakota's gross state product—the total value of goods and services produced each year. Retail businesses include grocery and clothing stores,

Bertin Gamble

Bertin Gamble knew how to make a sale. With his partner, Phil Skogmo, Gamble developed nearly 4,200 merchandising outlets in thirty-eight states and Canada. Beginning in 1925, the Gamble-Skogmo chain grew to be one of the largest retailers in North America. Born in Chicago in 1898, Gamble moved with his family to North Dakota as a child and attended school in Hunter. He met his future partner, Skogmo, there when he was only seven years old.

After finishing high school, Gamble worked in Minneapolis before returning to purchase an auto dealership in Fargo with Skogmo. They opened their first store in St. Cloud, Minnesota, and their second and third stores in Fargo and Grand Forks. Gamble was company president from 1925 to 1945 and board chairman until his retirement in 1977. The firm was acquired in 1980 by the Wickes Corporation, which is based in California. Bertin Gamble died in 1986. ■

restaurants, gas stations, video stores, telemarketing firms, banks, and real estate companies. Large medical centers are concentrated in Grand Forks, Fargo, and Bismarck.

State and federal government services also contribute to the state's economy. These include Native American reservations and air force bases.

Manufacturing

North Dakota's manufactured goods bring in more than $1.5 billion each year. Many of the state's products are foods, including bread, pasta, cheddar cheese, and ice cream. Sugar-beet refineries operate in several cities. Meat-processing firms produce hot dogs, steaks, and racks of ribs for barbecuing.

Harold Schafer

Harold Schafer is a far-sighted North Dakota business leader. In 1942, he founded the Gold Seal Company, one of the state's largest businesses. Gold Seal now produces Glass Wax, Mr. Bubble, and Snowy Bleach, among other home-care products for national distribution. Born in Stanton in 1912, Schafer graduated from Bismarck High School and attended North Dakota State University in Fargo. An active supporter of art projects, he was responsible for restoring the old town of Medora, and he also launched the popular Medora Musical Festival. Schafer was honored with the Horatio Alger Award, named for a fictional character who worked his way up from poverty. Schafer was also named to the Theodore Roosevelt Rough Rider North Dakota Hall of Fame in 1974. (His son Edward is now the governor of North Dakota.) ■

North Dakota also produces machinery and home-care products. Factories in Bismarck, Minot, and Wahpeton produce farm equipment. Aircraft parts and furniture are also important.

Communications

North Dakotans like to stay in touch with one another and the world. They watch television, listen to the radio, read newspapers, and surf the Internet. The state's first radio station, WDAY in Fargo, began broadcasting in 1922. KCJB, founded in 1953 in Minot, was its first television station. It is now called KXMC-TV. Today, seventy-five radio stations and twenty-five television stations broadcast in North Dakota.

The state's first newspaper was the *Frontier Scout*, published in 1864 at Fort Union. North Dakota now publishes about 100 daily and weekly newspapers and several dozen magazines.

Flying in North Dakota

North Dakota has 100 public airports. These airports are part of the state's interlocking transportation network of trains, planes, and buses.

On a daily basis, arrivals and departures of air passengers number around 8,000. Every year, more than 8,000 tons of cargo are shipped by air freight. ■

Bismarck Tribune

The *Bismarck Tribune*, started in 1873 by Clement A. Lounsberry, is the oldest existing newspaper in the state. One of the newspaper's reporters, Mark Kellogg, was killed in 1876 at the Battle of the Little Bighorn along with General George Armstrong Custer and his Seventh Cavalry troops. Lounsberry used the last words from Kellogg's tattered notebook to write an account of the battle. It was the first article about the military disaster to be published. ■

CHAPTER NINE

The People of North Dakota

A typical North Dakota resident is probably a mix of ethnic heritages. The 1990 census recorded numerous national backgrounds, including Arab, Austrian, Belgian, Danish, Dutch, Korean, Japanese, Native American, Norwegian, Polish, Swedish, and Swiss. For a state with such a small population, the diversity is exciting. Most people speak English, and some claim a Native American language as their primary language.

A North Dakota resident

During the first years of settlement, most people living in the region were French-Canadian, Scottish, British, Native American, or had a mixed racial background. By 1910, North Dakota had more foreign-born residents than any other state. Many early newcomers who farmed in the Red River valley were from Scandinavia, particularly Norway. Germans from Russia settled in the south-central part of the early territory and Germans from Germany settled all over the region.

By the 1920s, however, a majority of North Dakotans had been born in the state. This pattern remained consistent through the end of the 1990s. By then, 467,822 state residents were born in North Dakota, with 9,388 foreign-born residents and 156,949 citizens from other states.

Opposite: A wood carver at Norsk Hostfest

As the years pass and their links with Europe stretch over generations, most North Dakotans continue to follow their old European customs and Lutheran or Catholic religious traditions. These strong community ties help residents retain a sense of who they are and what they are about, even in tough times.

The state has strong Lutheran and Catholic traditions.

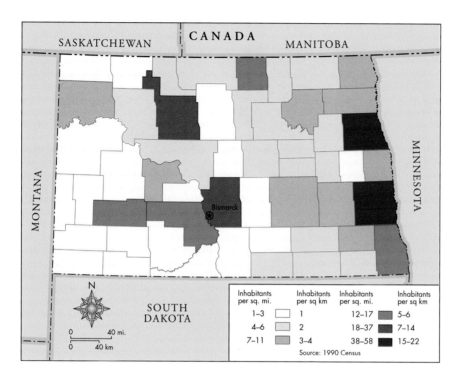

Inhabitants per sq. mi.		Inhabitants per sq km	Inhabitants per sq. mi.		Inhabitants per sq km
1–3		1	12–17		5–6
4–6		2	18–37		7–14
7–11		3–4	38–58		15–22

Source: 1990 Census

North Dakota's population density

Nevertheless, a large number of Native Americans continue to live in poverty on the state's four reservations. The rural and remote location of the reservations, the lack of job opportunities, the bad management by tribal and government officials, the poor schools, and inadequate health care make life difficult for the Native Americans who live on North Dakota's reservations.

Population

According to the 1990 census, North Dakota has 641,364 residents. According to government predictions, there will be 729,000 people living in the state by 2005. About 94 percent of the people are white, 4 percent are Native American, and fewer than 2 percent are African-American, Hispanic, or Asian and Pacific Islanders.

Celebrating the State's Heritages

North Dakotans preserve their heritage through festivals, exhibitions, and special events highlighting their ethnic origins. The Red River cities of Fargo-Moorhead host the Scandinavian Hjemkomst (pronounced YOM-comst) Festival each summer. Maypole dances, craft demonstrations, and foods entertain the crowds. Minot puts on a Scandinavian Norsk Hostfest each October. Icelandic State Park, 5 miles (8 km) west of Cavalier, honors the settlers from Iceland who originally farmed this section of North Dakota in the late 1800s. The Ukrainians celebrate their traditional foods and arts at a festival each year in Dickinson. Of course, wherever there are Irish, there is a St. Patrick's Day celebration. New Leipzig sponsors an Oktoberfest honoring its local German-Russian settlers.

Native Americans continue their long-standing traditions of powwows, dancing, drum songs, and arts on reservations and in towns and cities throughout North Dakota. Native American Days in Grand Forks celebrates the many Indian traditions. Bismarck is the site of a large international powwow every September.

Several museums, such as the Bell Isle Indian Museum in St. Michael, also celebrate the state's Native American culture. The Three Affiliated Tribes Museum west of New Town contains exhibits relating to the Mandan, Hidatsa, and Arkara heritages. In Belcourt, the Turtle Mountain Chippewa Heritage Center and Museum displays the art and crafts of the Chippewa. In Mandan, artisans work on jewelry, baskets, paintings, and sculptures at the Five Nations Art Museum—a restored Great Northern Railroad depot.

Population of North Dakota's Major Cities (1990)

Fargo	74,111
Grand Forks	49,425
Bismarck	49,256
Minot	34,544
Dickinson	16,097
Jamestown	15,571

Five Nations traditional jewelry for sale

A Rural Lifestyle

North Dakotans are quick to say "our people are our greatest resource." Most North Dakotans can trace their roots back to days on the farm, which gives the state a distinctly rural character. It wasn't until the 1980s that more people lived in towns than on farms.

In 1997, about 53 percent of North Dakotans were living in cities, up from 40 percent in 1990. Population experts say this trend is likely to continue as family farms decline and North Dakota develops more industry. Even by the end of the century, only seventeen cities had populations of more than 2,500. Only four had more than 25,000. The state's four largest communities are Fargo, Grand Forks, Bismarck, and Minot. They make up about one-third of the state's population.

Elementary Education

North Dakotans know they need a good education to achieve success. They understand that doing well in school can lead to great accomplishments later in life. This has been their philosophy since the beginning. Native American cultures incorporated learning throughout their lives, using the natural world as a classroom. On the other hand, the state's early settlers felt they needed a strong school system to promote learning.

In 1801, the region's first white settlement was established in Pembina. Settlers founded a school there in 1818. During territorial days, schools were run by missions, which ministered to Native Americans, mixed-race youngsters, and the few white children who lived in the region. The first legislative assembly met in 1862 and established a school system with James S. Foster as the territory's first superintendent of public instruction.

The North Dakota constitution of 1889 formalized the school system. At first, many children could not attend a full school year because they were needed to work on the family farm.

North Dakota has worked hard to strengthen the state's education system.

By the 1920s, however, most North Dakota youngsters graduated from high school. The state was hit hard during the Great Depression. Without income from taxes, many schools closed and many teachers lost their jobs. As the economy grew stronger in the 1940s and 1950s, the situation improved.

By the 1990s, the state's school system had developed an extensive system of certifying teachers and improving the quality of education. North Dakota is working to improve its offerings in technology, the arts, science, and business training. The state still has a way to go—its teachers' salaries are among the lowest in the United States.

By the end of the 1990s, there were 184 high school and 41 elementary schools districts in the state. Some 87,532 elementary and 39,880 high school pupils were enrolled. The North Dakota Indian Education Association ensures that Native American interests are represented.

University System

The state's extensive university system turns out thousands of highly rated graduates every year. Today, North Dakota has fifteen public and six private institutions of higher learning.

Six years before North Dakota became a state in 1883, the University of North Dakota in Grand Forks was founded by the Dakota territorial assembly. The University of North Dakota in Grand Forks, with some 11,499 students, is now the largest university in the Dakotas, Wyoming, and western Minnesota. The university's Chester Fritz Library has 2 million books and documents, making

The University of North Dakota in Grand Forks

In Space

North Dakota has three residents who have seen Earth from space. James F. Buchli (left) became an astronaut in 1979 and served on several space shuttle missions aboard the *Discovery*.

Geophysicist Anthony W. England was selected to be an astronaut in 1967, serving on the support crew for *Apollo 13* and *16* and aboard the *Challenger* space shuttle. After his space work, he became a mission specialist on the ground and now teaches at the University of Michigan.

Richard Hieb became an astronaut in 1986. A veteran of three space flights, he spent more than 750 hours in space, including 17 hours of walking in space.

Hieb took part in the first three-person space walk. On this mission, he orbited Earth 141 times in 213 hours. During the flight, he traveled 3.7 million miles (5.9 million km). On the space shuttle *Challenger*, Richard Hieb orbited Earth 236 times, traveling more than 6.1 million miles (9.8 million km). ■

it the state's largest library. The school also has a four-year medical school, a law school, and one of the largest aerospace training programs in the United States. Its students also take aviation training to become pilots throughout the world.

With its agricultural heritage, North Dakota offers many opportunities for students to study topics from horticulture to agrimarketing. The state board for vocational and technical education coordinates such classes at the state's college level.

Outside the formal school setting, the Future Farmers of America (FFA) has eighty-three chapters in the state with 4,200 members. This group helps young farmers train for today's farming industry. The state FFA convention is held each year on the North

Dakota State University's Fargo campus. It is a great time for young farmers to talk about their future and meet new friends.

The state's two-year institutions include the United Tribes Technical College in Bismarck, which began operating in 1969. The school offers occupational classes to several hundred students from a number of different Native American groups. Fort Berthold Community College, Little Hoop Community College in Fort Totten, Sitting Bull College in Fort Yates, and the Turtle Mountain Community College in Belcourt also primarily serve Native Americans.

David C. Jones

One famous military officer from North Dakota is David C. Jones. Born in 1921, Jones was raised in Minot and attended the University of North Dakota and Minot State College. He became a pilot in 1943 and worked his way up to air force chief of staff. He became chairman of the Joint Chiefs of Staff in 1978 and was reappointed in 1980.■

CHAPTER TEN

Authors, Artists, and Athletes

From Native American folk tales to today's novels, there is a long North Dakota tradition of storytelling. At the Dakota Cowboy Poets Gathering in Medora, men, women, and children in wide-brimmed Stetson hats, jeans, and chaps read their verses. The event is held annually over Memorial Day weekend, along with displays of Western art and a giant craft show.

Authors

Louise Erdrich, whose parents were German-American and French-Chippewa, grew up in Wahpeton, North Dakota, where her parents taught at a Bureau of Indian Affairs boarding school. She is the author of many award-winning novels, including *Love Medicine*, *Bingo Palace*, and *Tales of Burning Love*, all set in North Dakota.

Larry Woiwode, who was born in 1941 in Carrington, has written hundreds of award-winning poems and numerous novels and short stories. He now lives on a 160-acre (65-ha) organic farm near Mott, where he continues to turn out blockbusters such as

Cowboy poets in Medora

Opposite: At the United Tribes International Powwow

What I'm Going to Do, I Think and *Beyond the Bedroom Wall*. In 1995, the North Dakota legislative assembly named him the state's poet laureate.

Other poet laureates of North Dakota include David Solheim, an English instructor from Dickinson State University, Lydia O. Jackson, Henry R. Martinson, and Corbin A. Waldron. Another great North Dakota poet was James W. Foley, the state's first unofficial poet laureate in the early 1950s.

Louis L'Amour (1908–1988) of Jamestown was one of the nation's most prolific writers. He was author of more than 400 short stories and more than 100 novels, plus 65 film scripts. Most of his themes dealt with the Wild West. His books have been translated

Louis L'Amour wrote about adventures in the Wild West.

into twenty languages, and many were made into movies, such as *Hondo* starring John Wayne. L'Amour even wrote a volume of poetry, *Smoke from the Altar*.

Judy Baer from Cando, North Dakota, is a well-known and popular author of children's books. Her books include *Dakota Dream* and the multivolume *Cedar River Daydreams*.

Journalists

Several noted journalists called North Dakota their home. Edward Thompson, born in 1907, was raised in St. Thomas, North Dakota. He became an editor of *Life* magazine after a long career working for several newspapers. When he retired from *Life* in 1968, he served as special assistant to the secretary of state for Far Eastern affairs.

Era Bell Thompson (1905–1986) was the international editor of *Ebony* magazine. She wrote several books about growing up in North Dakota, including *American Daughter*. Her other books were *Africa, Land of My Father* and *White on Black*. While attending the University of North Dakota, she established five state women's track records and tied two international intercollegiate women's track records.

National television commentator Eric Sevareid, who grew up in Velva, was known for his essays on public issues and politics. He started working as a copyboy at the local

Era Bell Thompson on the cover of Ebony magazine

Television commentator
Eric Sevareid

newspaper when he was eighteen. Sevareid became a radio correspondent for CBS in 1939, covering World War II in Europe. He retired as a commentator for the network in 1977.

Love of Literature

The North Dakota Center for the Book, established in 1992, promotes and celebrates books and the state's literary heritage. The center runs many programs. Letters about Literature is an essay contest for youngsters six to twelve. Read*Write*Now! helps kids improve their communication skills. Literacy North Dakota works to teach adults how to read. In addition, the North Dakota Center for the Book hosts Tellabation, a regular evening of storytelling and lectures by North Dakota authors.

Theater and Actors

Theatergoers in North Dakota have many choices for first-rate productions, from school performances to professional shows. The Frost Fire Summer Theatre in Walhalla, the Fargo Theatre, and the Sleepy Hollow Summer Theater in Bismarck are professional theater groups. A 28-acre (11-ha) farm near Fargo is home to the Trollwood Performing Arts School, which hosts a summer program for young performers.

The state also has a number of noted performers. Dorothy Stickney, born in Dickinson in 1900, was an award-winning Broadway actress who starred in *Life with Father* and numerous other productions. In her early career, she traveled throughout the country to play in stock theater companies and vaudeville. Phyliss Frelich, born in 1944 in Devils Lake, won a coveted Tony Award for her role in Broadway's *Children of a Lesser God*. Deaf all her life, she always dreamed of becoming an actress and eventually helped found the National Theater of the Deaf.

A Frost Fire Summer Theatre production

Actress Angie Dickinson grew up in the town of Kulm.

Actress Angie Dickinson, born in 1932, grew up in the farming town of Kulm before moving to California. While working in a factory there, she decided to enter a beauty contest. A talent scout spotted her and got her involved in movies. Dickinson has starred in more than fifty films, with famous leading men such as John Wayne, Richard Burton, Marlon Brando, and Burt Reynolds. Dickinson is best known for her role in the television series *Police Woman* for which she earned a Golden Globe Award.

Native American dancing is theater of another sort. One of the largest dance competitions in the country, the United Tribes International Powwow, is held annually in Bismarck with hundreds of Native American contestants from Canada and the United States. The entrants perform with swirling feathers and jingling bells. When the announcer calls an "intertribal" dance, anyone can take part.

Powwows were originally held in the spring to celebrate the earth's new life. It was a time for Native Americans to meet old friends and celebrate. In the Sioux tradition, a powwow is also a prayer to Wakan-Tanka, the Great Spirit.

Art

Art museums are plentiful in North Dakota. Fargo's Plains Art Museum, the Hughes Fine Art Center at the University of North Dakota, and the North Dakota Museum of Art are renowned for their excellent exhibits. Minot State University's Northwest Art Center hosts shows by students and professionals. The Jamestown Art Center offers rotating art exhibits and performing-arts programs. Artists have a great chance to showcase their works at the Mandan Art Association annual art show, the Rough Rider International Art Show in Williston, the Prairie Arts Show in Dunseith, and the International Indian Arts Exposition in Bismarck.

Folk art in North Dakota includes quilt making, Hidatsa bird quill work, Polish paper cutting, and Ukrainian egg painting. The North Dakota Council on the Arts sponsors a traditional arts apprenticeship, ensuring that these crafts do not die out.

Quilt making can be a social event.

Ivan Dmitri

Among the state's most distinguished artists was photographer Ivan Dmitri (1900–1968). His works have been exhibited in most major museums in the United States and Europe. Dmitri, originally named Levon West, was the son of a traveling Congregational minister. After graduating from high school in Harvey, Dmitri studied business administration at the University of Minnesota, but he always kept his love of art alive and began etching famous personalities. Soon, his works were in great demand. To separate his artistic fields, he took the name of Ivan Dmitri when he became a photographer. ■

Music

The Medora Musical, a cabaret of songs and dances, is held every summer in the Burning Hills outdoor amphitheater in Medora. A Music in the Park big band series in Arvilla has been a famous North Dakota attraction for years. There is even an Old Fashioned Music Festival in West Fargo held each July in the Dakota Territory Dance Emporium. There are also various blues, bluegrass, and Bach concerts for those music lovers whose tastes run from pop to rock to classical.

One famous North Dakota musician was bandleader Lawrence Welk (1903–1992). He was one of eight children who grew up on a farm near Strasburg. He had to leave school as a youngster because of a long illness. While recuperating, Welk took up music, performing

Bandleader Lawrence Welk grew up near Strasburg.

at local dances to earn enough money to buy his first accordion. From there, he went on to star on radio and television with his Welk and the Champagne Music Makers.

Bobby Vee (born Robert Velline) was born in 1943 in Fargo. He started a rock-and-roll band in his garage when he was sixteen and went on to produce six gold records and record fourteen Top Forty hits.

Peggy Lee, an actress and singer, was also one of eight children. Born in 1920, she grew up in Jamestown and performed around her hometown as a child. She sang with such famous bandleaders as Benny Goodman, who appreciated her rhythm-and-blues style of music. Lee's talents earned her many awards as a recording star and film personality. She played the role of Lady in Disney's animated film *Lady and the Tramp*.

Sports

While there are no professional sports teams in North Dakota, the state has several famous sports personalities. From skiing to base-ball, the state has produced sports champions.

Casper Oimoen (1906–1995) was captain of the Olympic ski team in 1936. He won more than 400 medals and trophies over his long career and was inducted into the U.S. Skiing Hall of Fame in 1963. Oimoen was born in Norway where he learned to ski. After moving to North Dakota as a youngster, he took up ski jumping. In 1930, he won national championships. When he wasn't practicing his skiing techniques, Oimoen was a brick-layer. He worked on the construction crew that built the North Dakota state capitol.

It seems that almost everyone plays hockey in North Dakota. Cliff Purpur, whose nickname growing up was "Fido," took skating to the next level. He became the first Native American to become a National Hockey League player and one of the first Americans to play professionally. After playing for several clubs, he became a hockey coach at Grand Forks Central High School and the University of North Dakota.

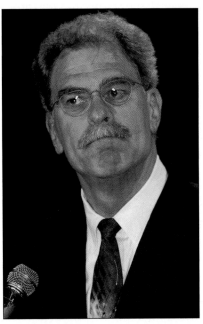

Phil Jackson made a name for himself as an NBA player and coach.

Phil Jackson grew up in Williston, where he was a fantastic basketball player. At the University of North Dakota, he earned All-American honors. In 1967, he was drafted by the New York Knicks. He led the team to a National Basketball Association (NBA) championship in 1973. Jackson went on to coach the Chicago Bulls and their superstar Michael Jordan from 1989 to 1998. Jackson's Bulls won an incredible six NBA championships in that time. After leaving the Bulls, Jackson was named coach of the Los Angeles Lakers in 1999.

The Roger Maris Baseball Museum in Fargo honors the noted North Dakota baseball great. In 1961, Maris (1934–1985) broke Babe Ruth's legendary home-run record, which had stood for thirty-four years. As a member of the New York Yankees, Maris hit sixty-one home runs. This was one more than Ruth's total in a sin-

Baseball great Roger Maris lived in Fargo.

gle season. In 1998, Mark McGwire broke Maris's record, hitting seventy home runs. Fargo, Maris's hometown, honors him with the Roger Maris Cancer Center, a Roger Maris Drive, and the Roger Maris Celebrity Golf Tournament.

Not everyone can be a sports hero. But North Dakotans still love to play ball, golf, hike, canoe, fish, ride horses, backpack, take dirt bikes into the woods, snowmobile, and hunt.

Timeline

United States History

1607 The first permanent English settlement is established in North America at Jamestown.

1620 Pilgrims found Plymouth Colony, the second permanent English settlement.

1776 America declares its independence from Britain.

1783 The Treaty of Paris officially ends the Revolutionary War in America.

1787 The U.S. Constitution is written.

1803 The Louisiana Purchase almost doubles the size of the United States.

1812–15 The United States and Britain fight the War of 1812.

North Dakota State History

600 B.C. Mound builders live in North Dakota.

Late 1600s The Cheyenne enter North Dakota.

1738 Pierre Gaultier de Varennes, Sieur de La Vérendrye, makes the first European exploration of North Dakota.

1803 The United States acquires North Dakota as part of the Louisiana Purchase.

1804 The Lewis and Clark expedition passes through North Dakota.

1812 The first permanent European settlement in North Dakota is established at Pembina.

United States History

The North and South fight **1861–65** each other in the American Civil War.

The United States is **1917–18** involved in World War I.

The stock market crashes, **1929** plunging the United States into the Great Depression.

The United States **1941–45** fights in World War II.
The United States becomes a **1945** charter member of the U.N.

The United States **1951–53** fights in the Korean War.

The U.S. Congress enacts a series of **1964** groundbreaking civil rights laws.

The United States **1964–73** engages in the Vietnam War.

The United States and other **1991** nations fight the brief Persian Gulf War against Iraq.

North Dakota State History

1837 A smallpox epidemic decimates the Native American population.

1861 Dakota Territory is created by the U.S. Congress.

1868 The Treaty of Fort Laramie is signed; the Dakota, or Sioux, are given land west of the Missouri River.

1889 North Dakota becomes the thirty-ninth state on November 2.

1890 Sitting Bull is killed on the Standing Rock Reservation.

1915 The Nonpartisan League is founded.

1951 Oil is discovered near Tioga.

1960 Garrison Dam is completed.

1980s North Dakota's rural population drops below 50 percent of the state's total population.

1997 Devastating spring flooding produces enormous damage in the Red River valley.

Fast Facts

State capitol

Statehood date	November 2, 1889, the 39th state
Origin of state name	*Dakota* is a Sioux word meaning "friend" or "ally"
State capital	Bismarck
State nickname	Peace Garden State
State motto	"Liberty and Union, Now and Forever One and Inseparable"
State bird	Western meadowlark
State flower	Wild prairie rose
State fish	Northern pike
State grass	Western wheatgrass
State fossil	Teredo petrified wood
State song	"North Dakota Hymn"
State tree	American elm

Soybean plants

State beverage	Milk
State fair	Third week in July at Minot
Total area; rank	70,704 sq. mi. (183,123 sq km); 18th
Land; rank	68,994 sq. mi. (178,694 sq km); 17th
Water; rank	1,710 sq. mi. (4,429 sq km); 18th
Inland water; **rank**	1,710 sq. mi. (4,429 sq km); 12th
Geographic center	Sheridan, 5 miles (8 km) southwest of McClusky
Latitude and longitude	North Dakota is located approximately between 45° 55' and 49° 00' N and 96° 32' and 104° 3' W
Highest point	White Butte, 3,506 feet (1,069 m)
Lowest point	750 feet (229 m) at Red River in Pembina County
Largest city	Fargo
Number of counties	53
Population; rank	641,364 (1990 census); 47th
Density	9 persons per sq. mi. (4 per sq km)
Population distribution	53% urban, 47% rural

Sledding

Ethnic distribution (does not equal 100%)		
	White	94.57%
	Native American	4.06%
	Hispanic	0.73%
	African-American	0.55%
	Asian and Pacific Islanders	0.54%
	Other	0.27%

Bismarck school-
children in the rain

Record high temperature	121°F (49°C) at Steele on July 6, 1936
Record low temperature	–60°F (–51°C) at Parshall on February 15, 1936
Average July temperature	70°F (21°C)
Average January temperature	7°F (–14°C)
Average annual precipitation	17 inches (43 cm)

Natural Areas and Historic Sites

National Park

Theodore Roosevelt National Park preserves scenic areas along the Missouri River as well as parts of the twenty-sixth president's Elkhorn Ranch.

National Historic Sites

Fort Union Trading Post National Historic Site was the site of a major fur-trading depot on the upper Missouri River from 1829 to 1867. Parts of the site are in North Dakota.

Knife River Indian Village contains the remnants of historic and prehistoric Native American villages.

State Parks

North Dakota maintains fifteen state parks.

Theodore Roosevelt
National Park

Sports Teams

NCAA Teams (Division 1)

North Dakota State University Bison

University of North Dakota Fighting Sioux

University of North Dakota in Grand Forks

Cultural Institutions

Libraries

The University of North Dakota (Fargo) has a complete set of the papers of the Nuremburg War Crimes Trial, which document World War II war crimes. It also holds a fine collection on the state's history.

North Dakota State University (Grand Forks) is one of the state's largest libraries and also houses a fine collection on North Dakota history.

The State Historical Society of North Dakota (Bismarck) has collections on the state's early history.

Museums

The State Historical Society of North Dakota (Bismarck) maintains numerous exhibits on the state's early history, American Indian history, pioneer life, and natural history.

The Geographical Center Historical Museum (Rugby) is on the site of the geographical center of North America.

Universities and Colleges

In the late 1990s, North Dakota had fifteen public and six private institutions of higher learning.

Winter

Annual Events

January–March

North Dakota Winter Show in Valley City (March)

April–June

Fort Seward Wagon Train in Jamestown (June)

Fort Union Rendezvous near Williston (June)

Old Time Fiddlers Contest at the International Peace Garden (June)

Medora Musical in Medora (June through Labor Day)

Native American dance

Special theme events at Trollwood Park in Fargo (June through Labor Day)

July–September

Governor's Cup Walleye Fishing Tournament on Lake Sakakawea (July)

Jaycee Rodeo Days in Mandan (July)

North Dakota State Fair in Minot (July)

Rough Rider Days in Dickinson (July)

Champion's Ride Rodeo in Sentinel Butte (August)

Pioneer Days at Bonanzaville, USA, in West Fargo (August)

Folkfest in Bismarck (September)

Potato Bowl in Grand Forks (September)

United Tribes International Powwow in Bismarck (September)

October–December

Norsk Hostfest in Minot (October)

Threshing Bee in Makoti (October)

Country Christmas at Bonanzaville, USA, in West Fargo (December)

Angie Dickinson

Famous People

Maxwell Anderson (1888–1959)	Playwright
Robert H. Bahmer (1904–1990)	U.S. archivist
George Catlin (1796–1872)	Western Indian expert and artist
Warren Christopher (1925–)	U.S. secretary of state
Ronald Davies (1904–1996)	Judge
Angie Dickinson (1932–)	Actor
Ivan Dmitri (1900–1968)	Photographer

Roger Maris

Carl Ben Eielson (1897–1929)	Aviator
Louise Erdrich (1954–)	Author
John Bernard Flannagan (1895–1942)	Sculptor
Bertin Gamble (1898–1986)	Businessman
Richard C. Halverson (1916–1995)	U.S. Senate chaplain
Harold K. Johnson (1912–1983)	Army general
David C. Jones (1921–)	Chairman of the Joint Chiefs of Staff
Louis L'Amour (1908–1988)	Writer
Roger Eugene Maris (1934–1985)	Baseball player
Casper Oimoen (1906–1995)	Skier
William Owens (1940–)	Admiral
Sitting Bull (1831–1890)	Sioux leader
Era Bell Thompson (1905–1986)	Editor
Lawrence Welk (1903–1992)	Entertainer

To Find Out More

History

- Black, Sheila. *Sitting Bull and the Battle of the Little Bighorn*. Englewood Cliffs, N.J.: Silver Burdett Press, 1990.
- Fradin, Dennis Brindell. *North Dakota.* Chicago: Childrens Press, 1994.
- Matthaei, Gay, Jewel Grutman, and Adam Cvijanovic. *The Ledgerbook of Thomas Blue Eagle*. Charlottesville, Va.: Thomasson-Grant, 1994.
- Nicholson, Robert. *The Sioux.* Broomall, Penn.: Chelsea House, 1994.
- Thompson, Kathleen. *North Dakota*. Austin, Tex.: Raintree/Steck Vaughn, 1996.
- Verba, Joan Marie. *North Dakota*. Minneapolis: Lerner, 1992.

Biographies

- Iannone, Catherine. *Sitting Bull: Lakota Leader*. Danbury, Conn.: Franklin Watts, 1998.
- Marvis, B. *George Custer*. Broomall, Penn.: Chelsea House, 1997.

Fiction

- Sneve, Virginia Driving Hawk. *High Elk's Treasure*. New York: Holiday House, 1995.
- Sneve, Virginia Driving Hawk. *When Thunders Spoke*. Lincoln, Neb.: University of Nebraska Press, 1993.
- Stewart, Jennifer. *If That Breathes Fire, We're Toast!* New York: Holiday House, 1999.
- Wilder, Laura Ingalls. *By the Shores of Silver Lake*. New York: HarperTrophy, 1973.

Websites

- **North Dakota Legislative Branch**
  http://www.state.nd.us/lr
  For information about the legislative assembly

- **North Dakota Tourism Department**
  http://www.ndtourism.com
  Complete information on what to see when traveling in North Dakota

- **State Historical Society of North Dakota**
  http://www.state.nd.us/hist
  Informative site on the state's history

Addresses

- **North Dakota Tourism Department**
  Tourism Department
  Liberty Memorial Building
  Capitol Grounds
  Bismarck, ND 58505
  For information on traveling in North Dakota

- **Office of the Governor**
  Director of Constituent Services
  State Capitol
  Bismarck, ND 58505
  For information on North Dakota's government

- **State Historical Society of North Dakota**
  Heritage Center
  612 E. Boulevard Avenue
  Bismarck, ND 58505
  For information on North Dakota's history

Index

Page numbers in *italics* indicate illustrations.

Meet the Author

Born in Iowa, Martin Hintz graduated from St. Paul's College (now University) of St. Thomas in Minnesota. He has written for numerous guidebooks, travel magazines, and newspapers. An award-winning author, he is a member of the Society of American Travel Writers, guidebookwriters.com, and several other professional journalism organizations.

Martin Hintz is often asked about his favorite destinations. "Every place I visit and write about has its own personality and charm. It is fun to learn about other people and their cultures. So take the time to talk with other people when you're on a trip," he says.

Preparation for writing this book involved visiting North Dakota, contacting libraries, reading newspapers, and interviewing many people in person and on the telephone. Hintz spoke with representatives of state agencies, political leaders, journalists, artists, authors, historians, children, farmers, business leaders, and educators to find out as much as he could about North Dakota.

Hintz also found the Internet to be a useful tool. "But finding your way through all that information can be difficult," he explains. "That is why reading books and talking to librarians and other specialists is also very important."

Martin Hintz lives in River Hills, Wisconsin, with his wife Pam Percy, a producer for Wisconsin Public Radio.

Photo Credits

Photographs ©:

AP/Wide World Photos: 115 (Cook), 126 (Damian Dovarganes), 89 (John Duricka), 124 bottom (Ho), 29 (Library of Congress), 122, 134 bottom (Susan Sterner), 38, 88 bottom, 118, 120, 127, 135
Chuck Haney: cover, 63
Corbis-Bettmann: 15, 28
Craig Bihrle: 8, 57, 64, 132 top
Dawn Charging: 7 top right, 56, 65, 68, 73, 109, 131 bottom
Dembinsky Photo Assoc.: 62 bottom (Dominique Braud), 61 (Rolf Kopfle), 7 bottom, 48 (Doug Locke), 2 (G. Alan Nelson), 90 (Richard Hamilton Smith)
Envision: 98 (Steven Needham)
Garry Redmann: 11, 84 top, 87, 95, 103 bottom, 111, 133 bottom
Gene Ahrens: 6 top center, 46, 70, 79
Jane Kurtz: 75
Kent and Donna Dannen: 52
Liaison Agency, Inc.: 13, 33 (Hulton Getty), 47 (Dan Koeck), 40 (L. Mayer)
Mary Liz Austin: 6 top right, 12
Minn-Dak Farmers Cooperative: 45
Minnesota Historical Society: 25, 101
NASA: 114
North Dakota Department of Transportation: 42, 44
North Dakota Institute for Regional Studies, NDSU Library: 102

North Dakota Secretary of State Office: 84 bottom
North Dakota Tourism Department: 59 (Dawn Charging), 22 (Pat Hertz), 71 (Cheryl Purdy)
North Wind Picture Archives: 21 (N. Carter), 26
PhotoEdit: 104, 105 (Barbara Stitzer)
Reinhard Brucker: 16, 91
Sheldon Green: 7 top center, 55, 74, 76, 77, 78, 97, 99, 103 top, 116, 117, 121, 123, 134 top
State Historical Society of North Dakota: 20, 23, 30, 31, 34, 36, 37, 41, 83, 88 top, 119, 124 top
State of North Dakota Governor's Office: 80, 82
Stock Montage, Inc.: 17 (The Newberry Library), 32, 39
Superstock, Inc.: 67, 106, 130
Terry Donnelly: 7 top left, 53
The Image Finders: 113, 133 top (Michael Evans)
Tom Till: back cover
Unicorn Stock Photos: 6 bottom, 85 (Robert E. Barber), 62 top, 132 bottom (Andre Jenny)
Visuals Unlimited: 100 (Tim Hauf), 92 (Doug Sokell), 93, 131 top (E. Webber)
Willard Clay: 6 top left, 9, 49
Maps by XNR Productions, Inc.